Between the Reins

A Continuing Journey into Honest Horsemanship

Between the Reins

A Continuing Journey into Honest Horsemanship

Tom Moates

978-09845850-1-4

Designed by Chris Legg

Cover photo by Terry McCoy

Dedication

To Carol, whose wisdom, support, and input was essential to the creation of this work—and whose fortitude and profound resilience continually inspire me.

Contents

Foreword

There is a saying that, "the last thing you learn is the first thing you need to know." I believe this is very true in horsemanship. So as we learn more, we can see, feel, and do a better job for our horses. Often, what is lacking that prevents a situation from working out better is simply something we have not yet learned, or at least not yet understood. How do we get there sooner? There's no substitute for experience. But that experience may actually come from someone who is sharing what they have done, the outcome, a meaningful explanation, especially from the horse's point of view. So that's where Tom Moates comes in. Once again, Tom has offered us a collection of his attempt at looking closely to improve his horsemanship. I mention the looking closely part because I think this is what causes many of you to become followers of Tom's writing.

Tom will mention to me one statement, phrase, or minor incident with a horse as if he had just seen it carved on the side of a mountain. Then comes all the whys, what ifs, connections to other things, and separations from other things as he begins to take a closer look at whatever it is. Often this causes me to look a lot closer at all the connections and implications that are in there--that I otherwise might just take for granted. I realize taking these things for granted is very wrong of me, so once again Tom will take me back to look closer to find more depth of understanding and clarity for people not so familiar with these thoughts on horsemanship.

Once Tom has a pretty clear understanding of something new, he's always itching to put it into practice. (Hold on horses, here we go again!) From these experiments and experiences we get the benefit of another good chapter for a book. We certainly appreciate his willingness to share the good, the questionable, and the wrecks so we might not have to repeat some of those same types of experiences.

So I hope Tom has once again succeeded at getting you to look closely at some of the thoughts he has laid out for us in this book. In your looking closely don't be surprised to find as you get clearer on a thought, it takes you back to things you thought you were clear on but now find them even more clear and useful to your horsemanship. This is, of course, the way it works. The last thing you may have just understood is the first thing you needed to know so you could really understand some of the first things you tried so hard to comprehend clearly. So good luck!

Thank you, Tom, for sharing your journey of searching for the next piece you really needed first. We hope you never find it if that means you keep sharing your journey with all of us, your readers.

Harry Whitney
August 2010

Acknowledgments

Harry Whitney continues to be an extraordinary mentor for my quest to get better with horses. More than that, he's a great friend and one whose advice I've been blessed to receive regarding many walks of life through some tough times in the past several years. Harry is a rock, both in and out of the corral, and sometimes having an example of how to be more rock-like serves me well in life. In a world full of questionable characters and dubious dealings, I've grown to have no doubt in Harry's honesty and integrity--and I've got a feeling this is part of what horses sense in him as well. This book, like the last, shares some of what Harry has taught me. I'm extremely grateful for his willingness to support these works in many ways, including writing the forewords! So thanks to Harry for everything he manages to accomplish.

A heartfelt thanks goes to Chris Legg, who is the graphic design genius behind the wonderful covers and layout for this book and the recently updated soft cover edition of *A Horse's Thought*. I couldn't ask for a better feel and look to these books, and his tireless hours putting them all together is appreciated more than he can know. More of his work can be seen at www.bluefinagency.com.

A special thanks goes out to the photographers who generously allowed me to use their great photos in this book: Tina Chagnon Anderson, Kathy Baker, Nan Barta, Ross Jacobs, Terry McCoy, Carol Moates, Ken Moates, and Pam Talley Stoneburner. Also, to Moyer Ministries for providing the image of Ronnie Moyer bull fighting. They all deserve a standing ovation for helping provide some visual support to the subjects I seek to explore in the text of this work.

Carol Moates and Diana Johnson put in quite a bit of editorial time on this manuscript. Their proofreading and editorial opinions are greatly valued. Also, I'd like to thank Suzy FitzSimmons, Catherine Millard, and Rita Riddile for their willingness to let me share some of their horses' stories in a direct way.

Emily Kitching has supported this work on many levels, including running a couple excerpts from it in her magazine, *Eclectic-Horseman.* She, along with her husband and partner, Steve Bell, also design, host, and update my website (www.TomMoates.com). I'm extremely grateful for their continued initiative to support and promote my writing. Much more on their extensive business can be found at: www.eclectic-horseman.com.

Holly Clanahan, the editor of the American Quarter Horse Association's membership magazine, *America's Horse* (www.AQHA.com), deserves a big thanks for her support of my work, and for arranging an excerpt from this book to run in that publication.

I appreciate the entire editorial staff at the AQHA, and their willingness to allow me to again present some of Harry Whitney's work to the membership.

(Tina Chagnon Anderson)

Introduction

Life seems to have whacked me with a barrage of particularly crazy changes over the past several years--with my wife Carol's two liver transplants topping the list. (I'm extremely pleased to report she's back on her feet and doing very well these days!) Working with horses remained one crucial constant for my sanity throughout this trying time.

Sometimes just knowing I needed to go out there and get the herd checked, fed, and watered proved to be a welcomed and therapeutic change of scenery. The basic care of the horses is a heartbeat of this farm, an essential activity needing daily attention without fail. There is something reassuring about that. Perhaps it harkens back to the formative years of my adolescence spent on a large dairy farm where I often was responsible for feeding cattle each day. It was a job requiring quite an array of tractors, silos, conveyors, loaders, and feed wagons. The responsibility included keeping close count and tabs on many different bunches of Holsteins spread out over hundreds of acres. Nowadays, even in two feet of snow or pouring rain, I still relish the daily up close moments I spend with our horses. Even better is when I work with them more extensively and get some positive changes. That kind of interaction with horses always sparks an inner glow in me. All of it made facing the other challenges in life recently less overwhelming somehow.

Writing about some of the amazing constructive changes I've witnessed and experienced between humans and horses with Harry's patient guidance is likewise incredibly rewarding. The work of recording those experiences is a gift to me in many ways. For one, it requires that a clear understanding take form in my mind to get down in words what I have witnessed and learned. The clarity that comes from this kind of writing then helps the lessons stick with me. There's no cheating when you go to put thoughts down on the page. It's all pretty clear to the reader if you've got something figured out or not, and the first reader is always the writer.

Between the Reins is a follow up to, *A Horse's Thought*. It builds on the work and stories started in that previous title. The response to that book has been fantastic. I'm very excited that recounting experiences that proved enlightening for me seems to help others gain insights into some aspects of horsemanship as well. I'm also extremely grateful Harry continues to be willing to approve of my presenting some of his teachings on the page.

Since the last book, Harry has criss-crossed America a few times and been to Australia teaching clinics. It is an arduous task to spend so much time on the road, and folks like me who benefit greatly from this unique life Harry lives are indebted to his tenacity to keep traveling and keep teaching. The upcoming schedule of Harry's clinics is always available on his website: www.harrywhitney.com.

Harry Whitney teaching a clinic hosted by long time friends and students of his, Ross Jacobs and Michèle Jedlicka, in Pakenham, Victoria, Australia. Ross is the author of a fantastic book exploring horsemanship through fictional stories entitled, *Old Men and Horses*. More on Ross and Michèle is available on their very extensive website and blog: www.goodhorsemanship.com.au. *(Ross Jacobs)*

On another note, two new equine characters have entered the narrative of my life since the last book. These two, Festus and Jubal, have quite a history and need a little introduction to help their entrances into the upcoming chapters make better sense.

Life's phases, since horses became a central part of my life, are now inextricably linked to which horses I worked with at various times. (I should add mules to that list in fairness since Kate the Mule represents a phase when she lived with us as well.) Festus and Jubal marked the beginning of the most recent era. These two large, sturdy American Quarter Horses came into my life through some exceedingly peculiar circumstances.

Tom with Kate the Mule back in 2006. *(Ken Moates)*

Festus and Jubal began their lives as ranch horses up around Montana and the Dakotas. Festus also spent some time as a back country guide's horse, and Jubal sometimes was used as a roping horse in rodeos. The geldings were bought by a fellow with basically no prior riding experience for a journey he planned to take across America from Canada to Mexico.

The series of events of how I came to own Jubal and Festus was put into motion when I was thinking about taking a long road journey on horseback myself (an idea I have since back-burnered). It's all quite a long story, but I'll keep it short....

I heard about this Canada to Mexico journey well before it started, and since the guy taking the trip was from overseas, I figured he might not be keeping the horses when he returned home. I tried to contact him over several months to see if I might arrange to get the horses after his trip ended. He never got back to me. Months later, he called me out of the blue. He had ended his trip in El Paso two weeks earlier, and now wanted to give me the horses if I'd take responsibility for them from that point on. They were boarded somewhere there in El Paso.

I was in no position to suddenly go trailer two horses half way across the country, or hire a mover to haul them to Virginia. The owner was unwilling to arrange or cover transport, and explained he was flying out of the country the next day.

Carol was still early in recovery from her surgeries, and it was Christmas time. However, I realized we had hay and pasture to accommodate two more horses if there was a way to get them here. Or, it might be possible, since I knew several folks in the south west, to arrange for them to be kept out that way for few months until I could figure things out. In truth, I felt these horses had performed quite a feat. Aside from the fact that they were along the lines of what I sought in a pair of horses at that time, I felt like they deserved some stability and proper care after completing such a journey.

In the spur of the moment I made a call to a friend of mine, James DeBord. James is a safety rider (pickup man) for the Professional Bull Riders (PBR) main tour and has a place in Yoakum, Texas. I thought he might be able to hold on to these horses for me for a short time, or know someone around El Paso that could. To my surprise, he explained he was going to come to Winston-Salem, North Carolina in about 6 weeks to work a PBR event, which is about an hour south of here. He'd be hauling his two horses in a stock trailer big enough to hold two more. Even better, the PBR event he'd be working before that would be in Dallas, and he thought a stock contractor would be coming to it from El Paso....

So that's what happened. In a strange series of connections, Festus and Jubal ended up mine. They were stabled in El Paso for over a month, picked up there by a bucking bull stock contractor, and made it over to the PBR event in Dallas where they hung out backstage with the bulls. When James was done working the event, he loaded them up with his horses and off they went to Yoakum for a stop over. Next it was east to Winston-Salem where Carol and I took our truck down, met up with James at the arena and loaded them up for the trip home to Virginia.

Many thanks to folks associated with the PBR who helped in this arrangement, and especially to James who was willing to put it all together and bring these horses along for the long haul. Honestly, if it hadn't been for James's confident reaction to my first phone call insuring me, "Oh...go ahead, I'm sure we can work it out..." those geldings never would have made it here. So, thanks James!

PBR safety rider, James DeBord, with Tom backstage before a bull riding event in Winston-Salem, North Carolina, just after loading up Festus and Jubal for the trip to Virginia. *(Carol Moates)*

Jubal (on the left) and Festus just upon arrival at our place in Virginia. (Tom Moates)

Festus and Jubal have opened new doors for me and presented new challenges, some of which I'm pleased to share in the upcoming pages. Harry even used Jubal as a saddle horse for his seven week stay in Tennessee at Mendin' Fences Farm this year... so the plot thickens! I hope this book provides plenty of fresh information for folks to chew on, and that it is helpful and fun.

Tom Moates
August 2010

Chapter 1

(Tom Moates)

Straightness

"Jubal!" I hollered.

Reflexes snapped my arms back, both reins in tow.

The enormous Quarter Horse barreled along at a powerful trot. I'd saddled him a little earlier with the intention of working on "straightness." Charging headlong into a tree was not exactly the

Harry Whitney. *(Tom Moates)*

kind of straightness I'd envisioned.

The gelding snapped awake at my yell coupled with the sudden pressure on the snaffle bit. (Yep...he *awoke* from being somewhere else mentally *while* trotting.)

At the last second, that horse dug in and stopped nose-to-bark right at the huge black locust tree. I very nearly went through the windshield and smashed into it anyway, and would have except for managing to clutch the saddle horn just as my mass began to catapult over his big beautiful head.

The situation was very nearly serious, but so absurd I laughed out loud realizing neither of us quite wrecked into the tree. The vision then came to mind of me as that cartoon Coyote being outfoxed by Road Runner and splatting against the mighty unforgiving trunk. Then I slither down to the roots into a broken-up puddle of parts as my trusty steed puts his head down and begins nonchalantly grazing—in his bridle of course.

Such a kamikaze close call I never care to experience again.

"How the heck," you might wonder, "did you nearly trot head-long into a tree bigger than the horse, Tom?" You might figure that between the rider and the horse, one of us could have noticed the forty-foot tall, four foot wide solid hardwood out there all by itself in the pasture. After all, there wasn't another obstacle in a hundred feet, with clear open grass all around. You might think we'd notice it getting closer and closer before we nearly smashed into it, right?

You'd be right too, if this was a "normal" situation. But this is my world, the Land of Tom, where "well trained" Quarter Horses arrive and then run into massive trees when asked to go "straight" *past* them in the open.

It is a really great lesson in retrospect. This odd situation, as it turns out, is one of the most perfect examples illustrating straightness and crookedness in a horse as explained to me by horsemanship clinician, Harry Whitney, that I ever experienced or witnessed. Harry and I began our discussion on the topic right after I'd re-read some of *True Unity*, a little book on communication between horses and humans by Tom Dorrance. It spoke of straightness and got me thinking about the idea when riding. That's when I went out to experiment with the idea and nearly trotted straight into that huge tree.

Tom riding a circular line on Jubal at Mendin' Fences Farm in Tennessee. *(Kathy Baker)*

Harry's sage advice over time began to provide a clearer picture to me of the relationship between the horse's mental and physical worlds, and how they overlap. Although his way of describing a horse's thought I'd grasped before in some situations (like if a horse's thought is in or out of a round pen when being worked, for example), this represented a whole new presentation of the concept for me. True straightness in a horse, and an understanding of how central it is to getting things really right with a horse, began to take hold in my mind in a more meaningful way at this point.

True Unity entered my collection of horse books at the beginning of my horsemanship journey. I read the book several times over a few years. It then sat collecting dust for at least a year before the episode with Jubal.

People often explain that the keys to unlocking the mysteries of horsemanship lay in layers between the lines of what is said in the book. It's not an intentional code. Rather, the simple observations and conclusions made by Dorrance are profound in their plainness. Particular significance can occur to the reader, so the belief goes, when one of these is read at the right time. In other words, if you've just thrown a leg over a new realization regarding some aspect of your relationship to a horse and then go back and read Dorrance, you may have a light bulb click on over your head. You couldn't have lit it up before because you weren't ready to see it. (In retrospect, and as a side note, I'm pretty sure that some of the folks so eager to point out these literary mysteries to me were in no position to have experienced such insights personally. They clearly had no light bulb on over their heads.)

The idea is a kind of Catch 22 deal—you don't catch what's being said if you don't have certain knowledge, but how to you get that knowledge if you can't understand what's being said? I guess the answer to the riddle ultimately is that the horse has to tell you. Get more proficient in speaking horse and then things start to jump off the page a little differently to the reader. This aura of mystique still perturbs me, but I'd be lying if I didn't explain that it does so because it proves to be true for me on occasion.

A fellow like Harry works "in the field" to impart some of what he's discovered to be true regarding bettering the relationship between horses and humans to others. That's the clinician's job, for sure. But, just like when working with a horse, it seems he can only set it up and then hope a person will stumble upon the flash of understanding. He can't just download it into another's brain. Just like Dorrance couldn't either.

Straightness beared out to be just this way with me. Simply stated, I was really struck by Dorrance's very keen articulation of the importance of straightness in a horse while being ridden. Likewise, his certainty of the very lopsidedness of horses caught me by surprise as well on my most recent re-reading.

It seems illogical at first. How can a horse *not* be straight? If a person climbs in the saddle and rides down the road, how bad can some crookedness possibly be? Especially if the rider hasn't even noticed it?

Dorrance's discussion of how horses are often not straight when ridden (a whole bunch of the time apparently by the way he talks) made me begin to wonder about my riding. It made me want to watch other riders closely to see, but that isn't easy since I don't see other riders often. I don't know if I ever really considered the question before this time. I'd read the same chapters in *True Unity* multiple times, understanding the words well enough, but never *considered* what he meant on this point in this way. I just read on through the discussion of straightness without there being any impact because its significance just wasn't there for me. Too many elementary things, like getting a feel for the reins or figuring out foot fall from the saddle, trumped any thoughts of more refined discussions. Getting forward, reverse, right, left, front quarters, back quarters, etc., took enough mental energy to sort out at that earlier time.

Handling those reins eventually became more second nature to me with the accumulating hours put in on horses. Feeling the horse's movements became increasingly apparent to me with experience as well. I don't mean to say I became expert in riding; I still haven't managed to come close to that. Synchronicity, however, or lack there of, between a horse and me while riding became much more evident through my improving feel of the horse. Essentially, I developed a better awareness of being a part of the whole—that is, I experienced a better familiarity of transitioning into a physical part of the rider/horse combined creature that exists when riding. Those physical demands began to dovetail into a new and more refined aptitude with me. During this time the moment offered itself up to think about straightness.

So, when I read in *True Unity*, "So many times even when people are working for straightness in a horse, they may think the horse is straight and it isn't," it made me wonder just where I fell on the spectrum of straightness. Actually, it made me figure since I was

Harry riding a straight line on Jubal in Tennessee. *(Tom Moates)*

oblivious to straightness existing in my horses at all, that things could be pretty horrible if I went looking.

I saddled the big sorrel, Jubal. The choice wasn't because I was picking on him as a good candidate for trouble. Three horses were getting my attention at the time. Niji, who's half-decade of shenanigans are well documented in much of my writing, and the two newcomers mentioned in the Introduction, Festus and Jubal.

Festus came with a knee injury. So, I picked Jubal just because it was time to get working on these Big-Uns, as I affectionately refer to them in plural, and the handsome fellow wasn't injured.

I'd put maybe four rides on the sorrel prior to this day. Already his autopilot response to take off at a quick clip before being asked to step off, or even getting my behind in the saddle, was mostly sorted out. Clearly, the equestrian traveler that had him before me stayed completely out to lunch, allowing this behavior to ingrain deeply. The horse increasingly must have felt a serious need to fill in for his own safety. It is to this very prolonged situation that I attribute Jubal's acute need to take over, send his thoughts to places other than with me and mine, and then attempt to take his body over where he projects those thoughts.

Harry and I enjoyed a hearty laugh over the phone that night when I recounted the afternoon's entertainment of exploring straightness. Of course, I explained how Tom Dorrance nearly wrecked my horse into a tree. It was the perfect segway into picking the clinician's brain on his view of the condition of straightness.

"A big part of crookedness in a horse is a plan of escape," Harry said, after he quit laughing. "A horse can't be with you and planning to escape at the same time...not the kind of 'with-you-ness' I'm talking about."

If the horse creates a plan of escape, then there is mental crookedness which also may manifest by a horse using his body unevenly. Harry gave the example of a little wooden toy train. Each train car behind the engine is connected by a string. When the whole thing is pulled by the engine, it tows right along as it should. However, if a child attempts to push the train forward from the caboose, the strings all go slack and the whole thing jumbles up into a big wreck. That, says Harry, is much like the relationship between a horse's thoughts, body, and us. If you can lead the horse's thoughts in a clear direction, the rest of the horse, body and all, line out nicely and you get a train heading right on down the tracks. If, however, you try to be the engine while the horse has another agenda and is pushing himself and you from his caboose, then the result may look a whole lot like a piled up old "Number 97." It is a derailed gnarly mess and certainly not lined up in a tidy fashion with each part following the other to get something accomplished.

Harry's keen observations of horses' thoughts and how they play into their actions long was a point of study for me before that big tree showed up. I saw easily enough how that notion worked in this example the minute he linked crookedness to a horse's plan of escape. I actually *felt* it when he said that over the phone. The afternoon's event was recent enough that I recalled the sensation of the gelding squirming away from my intended route. How his mind's desire to angle to the right absolutely drew his body that way as I asked for straight.

The line I wanted to ride went right along our established

trajectory at that moment leading straight along past the tree to the left. Jubal's thought already veered to the right and went off a ways in that direction. He merely wished to reunite his body with his mind (so basically, he lost his mind). Mind you, this whole thing unfolded in a half-acre pasture with his best buddy, Festus, standing right there not twenty feet away grazing contentedly. On our right, naturally. It wasn't like I was asking for a task that would be particularly crazy for any horse, let alone one who has seen more than fifteen hundred miles of America's motor highways and byways.

Simply asking something that miniscule—just to stay straight on line with my desired route for a hundred feet in his own pasture on a calm sunny day right near his buddy—represented a situation so troubling to Jubal that he could not do it. Obviously, this incongruity did not stem from my request being outwardly bloodcurdlingly scary or physically grueling. I realized Harry's wisdom, and saw the origin of Jubal's actions lay in a lack of confidence in the rider to look out for his best interests. It was about trust and giving up the position of "engine" on the toy train. He absolutely felt the need to escape my pesky interventions in his plans, and get back to where he sought safety.

Smack dab in the crotch of the invisible "Y" in the mental road, where the rider's thought went one way and the horse's another, there just happened to be (in the physical) a huge tree.

Neither my intentions, nor Jubal's, fully swayed his body as we barreled along. It became a crooked mess with inertia enough to continue plowing ahead at a good clip as we both sought to control our mutual direction. In fact, I distinctly remember his right eye and how it looked to his desired path. The intensity of his apprehension was so great, and his mind so completely elsewhere, it seemed he really didn't see that tree which was still right in his field of vision.

The colossal locust, however, put an end to the luxury of having time to sort out our differences of opinion. It provided a critical moment of decision. We floundered in between the two anyway, all the while moving forward.

BAM! There's a big fat unmoving tree.

I think he was just as alarmed as I was when we stopped right at it and the reality of our near wreck quickly sank in.

The situation viewed from the safety of a truck fifty feet away, looking at things unfold from the vantage point just behind the horse, no doubt would have been telling. Surely it would have shown Jubal's body twisted or curved as the gravity of his thought pulled him into one orbit, and I physically worked to keep him in another. This strong desire, potentially life-or-death in significance to the horse, spilled out in the direction of his thought with every cell he could manage. Even an inch closer to his desired destination was worth great trouble to that horse at that time. The length of his body had to show the yearning to commit to his own agenda. The spine could not have been straight, the ears could not have been forward, and the strength of the horse could not possibly have been coming through that off-kilter mental/physical locomotion. Loco-motion is a good way to put how it felt—that is: "crazy" motion.

"Actions are not separate from emotions in the horse," Harry continued. "Straightness in the horse isn't about the horse being straight exactly—it is about the horse being *mentally* straight. Work on mental straightness, and work to support straightness in the body, both. Since horses can't separate the two, both approaches will help to improve how the horse feels."

Not surprisingly, Harry brought my latest horse trouble back to asking how the horse feels about things. It is the epicenter of Harry's work with horses, and permeates all he accomplishes with them. When we are able to help improve how the horse feels about a situation, things obviously improve for us as well. Straightness follows naturally as a byproduct of the horse fully connecting with the rider. The two then can embody a single choice completely throughout their minds and bodies simultaneously.

In Harry's way of thinking, the horse even can be straight when he's bent. (How's that for one of those tricky, "well...it depends," horsemanship riddles?) Harry and I visited about this: if the rider imagines a line to stay on leading out in front of the horse and guides him along that way, and the horse follows that course in a continuous and unswerving way mentally and physically, the line can curve or go straight ahead—it doesn't matter. Either way the horse is still experiencing straightness. He is mentally with the rider, balanced, and prepared to commit to the unbroken course laid out by the rider. The situation is straight like the engine leading the toy train through a curve. The horse can be right with it even if you change your mind on where the line leads and then it goes any which way, even backwards. It is still straightness in the sense Harry described to me.

The horse is limited in his choices to affect a circumstance compared to the human. The main things a horse can do are flee from what is perceived as undesirable or move to a place he wants to go that he thinks is best and most comforting for himself at a particular moment. If that best place for the horse in his mind is unquestionably with us, mentally and physically, then no matter where we lead the horse he would rather be right there (wherever there with us happens to be) than anywhere else in the world.

I wonder if Jubal at that moment actually was drawn over to the right, and that was the deal? Were his thoughts with another horse, maybe Festus? Maybe he associated those few horses in the next pasture with comfort and safety, and so wanted to get his body over there? Or, perhaps, I was on his back asking to go in a direction he found uncertain, so he was just looking to flee from whatever I asked because I was asking *something*? Maybe my getting in the saddle and asking that simple request of him to follow along straight was all it took to take him back to some horrible experiences, and his dreadful feelings about my riding aren't actually the result of my dreadful riding? I'll never really know.

Thinking about these things, however, makes me more empathetic to the horse's plight. It sure gets me centered on working with his thoughts and trying different options to improve how he feels about various situations where trouble shows up. The horse, it seems, possesses little to change his own attitudes towards what bothers him. In other words, the horse certainly comes with some natural behavioral tendencies, but then reacts to experiences as they come along. He then builds up a lifetime of reactions so various rounds of cause-and-effect become proven in his mind to be positively true (like a human holding a rope beside him is going to whack him in the face at some random moment).

It seems the horse can't think beyond the places where he's stuck without intervention. That is where the clinic and clinician come in handy. Find those places where a horse is stuck and then get some help towards setting him up to get beyond it. The chances of the horse hanging out in the pasture at home and resolving the issues he has with human entanglements on his own are probably zero.

The human, on the other hoof, enjoys a wide range of creative tools to potentially alter the mindset of a horse if he learns to use them. It is the horse's God given capacity to trust a person on some level, amazing though it is after the treatment some endure at the hands of humans, which really makes any of what the human accomplishes possible. This foundation exists separately from any human endeavor. We're just lucky it's there. The fact that it is part of the horse's make up allows the thoughtful person to potentially get a horse to feel better about things. This in turn allows for the resolution of some issues, like not trotting head long into big trees (hopefully).

Work to get a horse more relaxed and willing and he not only feels better inside himself, but is certainly more safe, useful, fun, and pleasant for the rider as well. Discovering a problem exists is the first step towards fixing it—otherwise a person can't work on what he can't see.

That is the situation with Dorrance's book and Harry's words spoken at clinics. They've got no meaning until the person that really needs them sees that he needs them and how to apply them. The person needing a hand must develop an understanding of what those words reference, otherwise it is like someone speaking in a foreign tongue. Japanese words have plenty of meaning to those who are familiar with that language, but I can't comprehend a word of it. But, a person can go take a course on a language unfamiliar to him and soon begin to catch some of it. Stick with those studies, go live among native speakers of that language, and then you eventually will begin to get pretty fluent. As I've heard Harry say many times about people and their horses, "You can't see it until you see it, then you wonder how you never saw it before."

Well, believe me, I saw it that day in the pasture with Jubal. The word "straightness" entered my vocabulary in bold type. Getting around to experiencing some traction towards resolving crookedness was another matter altogether. Good thing there's a whole book left here to explore this. I'm going to need it!

Chapter 2

(Kathy Baker)

The Trampoline Factor

Oh man...the ride was going great! Niji and I traveled for a quarter mile from the house out along the farm road. I dismounted, tied the sorrel gelding to a hickory tree, and fed Carol's Paint stallion, Chief, who lives in our upper pasture. Riding Niji to do my feeding chores around the farm was a long standing ambition of mine, one which presented big troubles every time I left the confines of a corral to give it a try.

The gelding stood there calmly by the tree, which was never a sure thing, and made me feel very optimistic. Then I untied him, remounted, and decided since things looked so good to head out and ride a little further. I decided to try going out onto the single lane gravel county road a ways.

Yappy little dogs barked their fool heads off and charged us, which the sorrel handled stoically. Add to that a squirrel, a rabbit, and some cows...the gelding did fantastic! After a mile or so, I stopped him and sat there, released a deep breath, and looked around from the saddle grinning. It wasn't the first time we'd ridden this road, but so far it proved to be one of the best.

The sky at this stretch of road opens up from the more enclosed wooded area of our place. Fields on both sides let the vast expanse of farms and forests stretching over a sizable span of the Blue Ridge mountains come into view. Niji perked up with interest at this sudden openness. The gelding looked around a bit wide eyed, not having ventured out of his valley home in months. Exploring further would have suited him fine, it seems. I, however, felt ecstatic at the progress of this simple ride into unusual territory. I decided not to push our luck by going on further that day, and hoped to preserve the positive experience to build on next time. The goal, after all, was to get a permanent improvement with this horse so such rides become the norm, not an exception.

Surely on the ride out we'd seen every challenge from where we now stood back to the house. Heck, there were only two houses between there and Chief, and what could be more hostile and unsettling than those yippie miniature pincher dogs?

Retracing our hoof prints in a section of road with more dirt than gravel, we entered back into the forest. As we approached the clearing with the dogs, now on our left, I decided to dismount. I hadn't planned on it, and don't remember a particular thought process leading to the decision. By some reflex, I just suddenly felt inclined to dismount and lead Niji. The lawn provided a nice footing, so I circled the horse around me a couple of times for a little groundwork along the way, which went well.

The yappers trailed us again at this point, without incident, into a large empty stretch of yard. I saw the neighbor's kid over on a great big trampoline way across the lawn, at least a hundred feet away, at the edge of the woods. She was just stretched out on it. I waved, she waved, and then she stood up and jumped on it.

Now, I've been around horses exploding. I've seen a horse jump out of a pen made of extra tall panels when a tumble weed blew in off the desert. I've seen a horse rip the lead rope out of the hands of a person trying to introduce a flag and go tearing off like a lunatic. Niji lost it as bad as any horse I'd ever seen when she jumped.

I was not prepared, but barely managed to hang onto the very end of the lead rope, somehow.

Clearly, the attention pleased the little girl. So, the vixen jumped higher and then started doing flips. Niji flipped right out with her. He reared. He bolted in circles around me trying wildly to pull the rope loose from my grip. He kicked. He went bezirkers. There was no settling him.

The girl thought it was hysterical, and put on all the more of an acrobatic show the whole time.

I tried to get Niji back with me, to use the situation as an opportunity to work through the new strange stimulus and get back to me mentally, but it was no use. I couldn't get big enough or hang in there long enough to overcome the trampoline factor. I retreated with him still snorting and being a fire breathing dragon all the way into the road. He didn't settle down until we were near Chief. What a change from two minutes earlier!

After the incident, I jotted down "The Trampoline Factor" to be a title for an essay. "What a great lesson," I thought at the time, "that even when your horse is going great, such oddities as a kid on a

Tom works with Chief in his pasture. *(Ken Moates)*

trampoline can send him over the edge."

The morals of the story would be: never forget to keep the unexpected in the back of your mind when out working with your horse, and to work in controlled environments to push your horse's envelope and find anything and everything you can which might set him off. The more stuff you find that bothers him and that you familiarize him with, surely the more he'll look to you for confidence, and the fewer kinds of situations will remain that might flip him out.

But, then I tried to ride Niji up the farm road to Chief the next day. It went horribly. That gelding decided as we went along the road to suddenly veer off course. He wanted to go visit some other horses in a pasture to the right. I couldn't seem to avoid this from the saddle. I reined. I used my legs. I spun him in circles and then tried to release pressure and get him headed my way. I even got down and remounted with a limb in my hand to try to use it like a flag and put a little visual pressure up by his eye to help keep him lined up on where I wanted us to go. Nothing worked, and we spiraled out of control with neither of us getting where we wanted to go, and ending up on a very steep hillside with terrible rocky footing. When it got way too dangerous, which didn't take long, I dismounted and led him away feeling further than ever from my hope of riding this horse around the farm safely.

More than anything, it perplexed me that just the day before the basic ride through this spot went so well. This area posed no problems as we breezed past it. Now, the very next day, what was working for us before flew completely out the window. Even after getting down and walking him back onto the farm road, remounting, and heading back up towards Chief, the crazy sorrel started walking off the road again. It brought me to the end of my rope. I was out of tools to cope with his unrelenting side tracking. It seemed especially baffling since I felt certain Niji knew what I was asking of him. There had been so much riding in the confines of corrals that the cues for right, left, forwards, and back at the very least were perfectly clear to him. To make matters worse, in my mind it made no sense for this horse to desire to leave the nice road for a horrendous ditch.

I dismounted, did the best job I could muster to contain my anger and frustration which began to spill out in the form of verbal threats, and led him up the road. There was no trouble when leading him. The battles only began when I tried to ride him.

Twice before, this very behavior (not the trampoline, but the running off the road bit) surfaced between Niji and me. I developed various theories as to what was going on. Some were more over-intellectualized than others, and my answer to all of them ultimately ended up being just to return to the round pen and start over from the beginning with the gelding in the tiny world of that corral. I figured ultimately I missed something along the way ("duh, yuh think?" I can hear Niji saying to himself), and I might get it covered with another go at starting again with all that ground work, saddling, riding in circles, etc. This approach, just for the record, Carol classifies as insane: i.e., doing the same thing over and again hoping for different results.

It was rather a shotgun approach to solving a horse problem, I admit, hoping to stumble onto the answer by starting over again rather than by working on the problem as it presented itself to be worked on. I, however, did not yet posses the skills to deal with this trouble. Harry, no doubt, would say something profound about this (after first agreeing with Carol's evaluation of my mental state) like I mentioned in the first chapter, "until you see it, you can't see it, then when you see it, you wonder how you never saw it before." Not a particularly instructionally helpful insight for this mess I was in at the moment, but pretty hard to refute. It does, I suppose, at least point to the optimistic fact that: other ways to fix a horse problem, which will work, but that you can't access, do indeed exist out there to be seen in the future, if you live long enough to get there.

In fact, it was this very riding issue with Niji that ultimately pressed me to seek the help that eventually led to getting some of it sorted out, and provided me the very tools I lacked. The challenge improved me as a horseman, but only after a really long grueling lesson. It is one that I enjoy a better grip on now so that I can recognize similar situations in other horses like Jubal and Festus, and I still face it at times even with Niji. Notice how Niji at first was straight for much of the ride that first day, but then the downward spiral manifested in increasingly less straightness. The situation is not unlike Jubal and me nearly kissing that big tree. This trouble with Niji, however, was well before Jubal entered my life.

The result in the immediate aftermath of the trampoline incident, however, was that I didn't write the essay about the trampoline factor. How could I when suddenly the answers I thought I'd discovered were swept away the next day into a tepid sea of equine mis-behavioral despair? Sounds like a disorder...EMBD. It certainly proved so for me at the time.

I wondered if the trampoline situation caused our regression to this other trouble? After all, it seemed not to be present just before the incident of the previous day. Then again, I couldn't explain why spooking at the trampoline would produce any influence on just basic riding down the road with Niji. It didn't seem to fit. There still seemed to be a good lesson in that trampoline deal anyway, but the big picture now looked quite hazy.

Unable to separate the truth of the matter in this muddled maze of equine misfit behavior from the uncertainties, I felt unqualified to write on either the trampoline factor or the puzzling degradation from a nice ride on the road one day to Niji's indecipherable actions causing acute episodes of EMBD the next. To make matters worse, after waiting for another day hoping the air might just clear miraculously somehow on its own (to further test Carol's insanity theory), I attempted to ride Niji again up to Chief. The side-tracking increased and intensified. In fact, soon we could not get out of the paddock and to the road before he started that dreaded hijacking of the ride to the left and right off my intended path. I didn't understand it, but realized all too well that to keep going like this without getting things heading in a better direction only strengthened the opposite in him of what I sought.

So, I headed into uncharted territory yet again. To make a long story short, I found that I lacked the ability to tell when Niji left me mentally. After getting some help from Carol and our friend, Terrie Wood, to watch me ride him and report in on what they saw, it shocked me to find out Niji's mind left me about every two steps! Literally.

Now, the good trip up the road before the trampoline accident stuck like a thorn in my saddle blanket. How, if Niji was *never* with me for more than a few feet as I discovered, could the ride out the road that one day for at least half a mile been so incredibly good? That inconsistency just drove me nuts. What did I have working for us then to keep the horse with me mentally? And, how was it now so lost that it could not be recovered for even five steps? I pondered this for quite a few days while working to improve on the newly found trouble. It finally became apparent.

To check in with Niji and see where his thoughts were, I began to put slight pressure on a rein. When riding, if he was looking to me mentally, he'd react by tipping his head over to that side slightly. If not, I'd discover easily enough that he'd be committed to his own agenda by not reacting, bracing, or even just lacking softness to the slight request.

If he was gone, I'd do something with him like disengage the hind quarters, back up, or bump to a trot to get his thoughts back with me. We did a lot of that kind of thing. Honestly, it may be hard to believe, but there were more of these exercises than forward steps for the first few rides. That is just truly how far from being with me Niji was. It is also how far ahead of the trouble the rider needed to be with this horse—that is, by the time I noticed the horse's hostile takeover in big actions, those obvious symptoms resulted from a situation already long in motion. A more refined horseman than me would pick up on those early warning signs and get the horse's thoughts back with him long before the big obvious trouble ever took root. Lack of a soft response to a rein is the same trouble as the horse veering off the road into a ditch against the rider's desire, it's just magnified.

Working with this scheme, I recognized that sometimes it was obvious when the gelding took over, like when he took a sharp turn off the road against my better judgment. But many times, the only way to know his thoughts were gone elsewhere was to do a rein check. Then it finally made sense—since I lacked the ability to discern if the horse was with me or not unless a huge action was involved, if Niji's thought just happened to be lined up going to the same place I wanted to go, I didn't realize he wasn't with me. In fact, it seemed like the best ride ever, since we were in a sense "together." I couldn't tell it really was only as two completely separate individuals whose intentions by chance overlapped at that moment in time. The great ride out the road before the trampoline incident was exactly an expression of this situation. Niji was no more with me on that ride than when we were over a ditch and up a bank somewhere. I just didn't know the difference because at that point he just happened to want to go along the same road I did.

What a curiosity to see that a horse's actions don't necessarily mean what they might seem to be at first. It requires substantial probing into what is going on with a horse, as well as developing our own ability to see where the horse's mind is, to get through such tough spots. The horse, however, always tells us. But, before we have the pieces of the puzzle in place to understand his language, we may easily misinterpret his message. "Until you see it, you can't see it, then when you see it, you wonder how you never saw it before."

This relates to mechanical control of horses also. Tying a horse's head down or using an aggressive bit to force your will on the horse may get the horse where you want him physically. Some folks might even breath a huge sigh of relief and think that is finally the answer they've been looking for. But, the horse mentally may be somewhere quite different than with you, even if he seems physically to go how and where you want him to. If you seek a horse truly willing and on the same page with you, difficulties must be understood and worked through for better understanding and an improved relationship, not just mechanically altered. Physical control over the horse in place of mental companionship and understanding only confines the horse to fewer choices. It's like putting the rider in a straight jacket and back brace—does that make a person feel happy

Niji and Tom on the farm. *(Carol Moates)*

to be in the saddle in that physical position?

It took weeks of diligent work to ride that gelding a hundred feet without him taking over and checking out on me. The mental nuances I needed to pay attention to were way finer than anything I'd cued into before. There were tons of little things to watch for and work on right in front of me, and had been since the beginning. I just lacked the right situation to bring it to my attention. Still, it would be many months later when I trailered Niji to a horsemanship clinic in Hanover, Virginia with Harry and rode all week before I'd fully appreciate how pitiful my capabilities were at keeping that horse with me. After that week of intensive work (and trouble, and breakthroughs) we entered a whole new phase that remains very productive. Now I'm able to enjoy riding around more area here on the place without Niji taking the reins. Riding to Chief's pasture and back remains a good exercise in "where's Niji's thought?" but we don't end up in the bushes or down the mountainside these days.

So, with greater understanding and confidence, probably two years later at this point, I feel I can reflect on that day of the trampoline incident and share what I believe occurred. And, finally, present what I think is the trampoline factor.

The trampoline factor is the primer charge that ignites a big explosion in your horse, unexpectedly, which reveals where your relationship with the horse is lacking.

On the one hand, a kid doing flips on a trampoline might be so bizarre as to spook almost any horse. But, a horse that is with you in the Harry Whitney sense will spook then immediately look to the rider to see what to do. It is automatic because the relationship, communication, and willingness all are real, solid, and real solid. On the other hand, a horse like Niji, without a concrete confidence in the human's lead spooks and mentally melts down attempting to take over the situation as the rider works to get through to the panicking horse and have a say.

I suppose one does well to remember that to the human's brain, the situation is a relatively simple matter. "Oh...there's a kid on a trampoline, ha, weird yes, but let's just move away from the trampoline and everything is alright," one thinks. The horse, however, may lack a reference of experience for something that strange. So it literally becomes a moment of life and death potential for him. It engages his hardwired flight response, and that is why the reaction, as I experienced with Niji, becomes so incredibly strong.

To develop an appreciation of how the horse is feeling in an EMBD episode goes a long way to dissolving the anger and frustration we might feel towards the horse in such a situation. The horse isn't wrong, he is merely doing the very best he can given the sum total of his make up and experiences.

It isn't up to him to figure it out and get right with a person. It is up to a person to get better with the horse and help him to understand he can count on us in every situation—the ones we can plan for, and even the ones we can't anticipate: like a flipping kid on a trampoline!

So, I've got a couple really great examples of un-straightness and downright crookedness shared...so now it's time to have a look at how some of this finally improved.

Chapter 3

(Tom Moates)

Thought Magnets

Some equine thought magnets aren't very difficult to detect. The gate of a round pen is a perfect example. Take your horse into a round pen and simply ride in a circle staying three feet off the fence.

If you feel the horse press a shoulder over and want to arc to the gate, or slow at the gate...or maybe even stop at the gate, that's the draw of a thought magnet. The horse's thought is attracted to that gate like metal to a magnet, and his body likewise gravitates towards it.

Such thought magnets can pop up in many places with the horse, and they are one underlying cause of crookedness. Like with Jubal and the big tree and Niji once he started veering off the road, a horse can't be thinking about getting away somewhere else and be really with you at the same time. Under Harry's definition of straightness, a horse can't be straight if asked to do something while in the grip of a thought magnet. His mind is at best split between you and something else, and his thoughts may be gone elsewhere altogether. Stated another way, the thought magnet is a place or thing that not only draws the horse's attention, but his desire and body as well. A mental sidetrack of this magnitude in turn blots out much or all of the human's communication with a horse at the time.

A car pulling in and stopping nearby might cause your horse to turn his head and look, for example, but not produce in him the desire to take his body over to that car. Just checking out a sudden change in the environment and then turning attention back to the person is not the kind of situation I'm referring to. In fact, awareness and curiosity in a horse are really good things. You want the horse to be awake and sensitive to his surroundings and take some responsibility for his, and your, well being. However, substitute that car with a horse and rider and then your horse might not just want to check out the change, but become very intent on going over to meet the equine newcomer. Or at least find himself unable to break away from the other horse mentally to turn back to give full concentration to the person working with him.

It is this kind of draw and desire that gets in the way of the horse being fully committed to following a person's lead. Intervention on the human's part is probably the only way to improve

Kathy Scott and her mare, Miss Molly, just outside the fence provide a perfect thought magnet for an Arab gelding as Charity Przepiora attempts to gain his attention with the flag at a clinic at Fitz Farm in Eagle Lake, Minnesota. *(Tom Moates)*

the relationship between human and horse so that thought magnets hold far less grip on them. The desired outcome is to get a horse feeling better in general, and especially so when with you.

There are any number of actions to choose from that might loosen the grip of thought magnets on a horse. Really, the action itself is not all that important. Backing the horse, circling him around you, or acting like a nut right in front of him all may be equally effective. Simply taking action and doing something that gains and holds the horse's attention is the beginning of changing the horse's focus. If you are of little importance to the horse, then any thought magnet more significant than you is going to dominate the horse's consciousness. If you are more important and reassuring to the horse than anything in the area, then you have his attention first and foremost.

Harry tips a horse's thought. (Tom Moates)

Harry makes a critical point about getting this sorted out; breaking into the horse's mental world is only half the equation. Then you must lead him somewhere along with you once you are on his radar.

In other words, by breaking the connection between thought magnets and the horse we interrupt a way he has developed to seek a kind of comfort in various situations. Some horses can project their thoughts very strongly to other places hoping to find consolation. They do this even though they actually ruin their chances of serenity (simply being happy right where they are) in the process. If we block that defense mechanism but provide no alternative purpose beyond it, then we potentially leave the horse in a bigger void and less comforted than he was on his own.

The desire in the human should be to get a horse feeling better about things. If a thought magnet draws a horse to somewhere else, it means that place represents a longing in the horse to get to some other place. He wants to feel better, which in turn means he isn't confident in his present situation. If he wants to feel better by going over there then he already is trying to fill an emotional void inside himself over here.

If you block thought magnets, but offer no better deal in trade, then the horse is no better off. He may even lose what confidence he has in the human. He might begin to feel really boxed in and get resentful. This may be amplified if mechanical devices are used to position his body without developing a better understanding so he willingly moves his own body in line with a request.

There is timing involved in this type of communication. Timing is tough to discuss in print. It can be difficult enough to grasp in real time with Harry right there offering suggestions. Essentially, you block a wayward thought in the horse through an action, support him for redirecting it to you, and have something in mind for him to do with you that instills confidence in him. Keep in mind the responsibility that comes with your actions when you are around a horse and trying to shift his full attention to your line of desire. Those actions may produce lasting affects, and all care should be taken to make them positive building blocks for the horse.

Which brings us to the point of intervention. Niji was the king of thought magnets. Once I began to see how often and rapidly his attention went elsewhere, I likewise realized my presence by comparison was of very little consequence to him. This proved true both riding and on the ground.

We rode in a week long horsemanship clinic with Harry in Hannover, Virginia in 2008. It was there that the full force of our mental troubles manifested clearly to me once and for all. It proved to be one of those deals that I've endured several times...everybody else in the entire clinic is having a group ride around in an outdoor arena and Niji and I are still all over the place in the mix just trying to get a little ground work done. Don't forget this is a horse who at times has been worked on the ground and ridden without much trouble at home over quite a few years. So I'm on the ground there just asking the gelding simply to circle me on a lead rope *while* paying attention to me. When I'd insist he hold his attention on me, he'd blow a gasket. He would kick, romp around, and go crazy. Keeping his focus from wondering was the crux of the trouble. It is a point that I never fully comprehended before.

Honestly, if I asked Niji to go out on the end of the lead

and circle me right there in the clinic, but allowed him to be mostly attentive to the horses all around, he'd be pretty decent. However, ask him to go out there and circle me with his full attention *on me*, and we had a major battle on our hands. It sounds bizarre, but being able to let his attention draw to his mental magnets was so important to Niji that blocking those thoughts caused a physical eruption in him. I was forced to get really big to get his attention in the first place—jumping, making noise, shaking the rope—and then he often just took off! It was all I could do to hold that rope and get him turned back my way. This went on and on and on. I hardly had the reserves of energy required to keep insisting he pay attention to me until there was a more lasting change in him. Improvement, however, finally started to enter the picture. Harry tag teamed him with me

Harry races on Jubal (who's hidden from view) to flag Stoney and get a change of thought at a clinic in Floyd, Virginia. (Terry McCoy)

a couple of times which helped a great deal. Still, the change came very slowly for the gelding and me at first. It took quite a bit of time to see it start to stick.

These thought magnets of Niji's in the arena shouldn't have been any big deal in my mind—horses being ridden in circles mostly, a few loose in a paddock just over the fence, and nothing all that exceptional. I developed an appreciation, however, that this horse exhibited a very deep need to keep track of it all. I think he mentally was figuring on how to line out the whole bunch to suite his requirements. He might have started working on it too if it weren't for that lead rope stopping him, along with my pesky requests buzzing in his mind like a fly in his ear.

Ultimately, a positive and more lasting change came through with Niji. It just demanded an enduring consistency with the groundwork in the arena. Time after time I snapped Niji's attention back as it started to slip away. Time after time I'd get in there and rub and praise him when he'd manage to work a little while keeping with me mentally. After getting a tiny hold on breaking the grip of the thought magnets on him, it became possible to build on the modest start. Eventually he came around to feeling better about focusing on me and my request rather than fretting about all those other horses. It boiled down to just a bunch of work. Just hanging in there with the dust flying, getting jerked around on the lead rope, and trying to be absolutely consistent over and over.

This situation could be seen in terms of pressure and release. I applied pressure to break the spell Niji was under, calling his attention elsewhere. When the gelding gave up those thoughts and came around to me and mine, I let him feel an instant release and encouraged him to stick with me there for a bit relaxed. Then I'd ask for a little something from him again, like backing a few steps or going out into a circle around me. I worked to keep the better deal going as long as he stayed with me while undertaking the task, but amped up some pressure the second (or second before, if I could see it coming) he began to leave me mentally.

However, "pressure and release" is a phrase I'm a bit weary of. It oversimplifies the complexities involved in breaking the hold of thought magnets. I hear the saying brandished often and immediately begin to visualize someone poking a horse in the hide to get him to move and then releasing the poke. Harry brought about a whole new way of thinking about this concept for me, which I prefer to keep foremost in mind. Instead of "pressure," which might be misconstrued as a crude physical pressure, the idea of "blocking and redirecting a thought" seems more applicable and preferable. Just asking the horse something as simple as backing up a few steps may be enough to bring his thought back to us. Sometimes getting a little big may be necessary. Regardless, if we manage to block the offending thought and offer a new route for the horse to think along which fosters clear understanding and the comfort of our confidence and support, we help the horse to feel better inside. It shouldn't take too long before he realizes that more pleasant situation is the one he prefers. Human intervention can bring about this kind of positive change when done correctly, and it is amazing to experience.

The work on the ground with Niji finally shaped up pretty well at this clinic. The shift was obvious. After a couple of days he started to look to me by default much of the time when on a lead rope. If a thought magnet drew his attention elsewhere, he was much less committed to it and I had to do very little to bring his thought back my way. He became much more relaxed in the groundwork, regardless of what was going on around him or what I asked of him. Then, I felt it was time to mount up and ride the gelding among the others during a group ride in the outdoor arena....

Chapter 4

(Terry McCoy)

Niji Bolted!

Niji bolted!

The instantaneous acceleration to a furious gallop found me shocked in the saddle. Surprised, I endured being swept along so sharply even my adrenaline rush faltered three strides behind us. The sorrel gelding charged between horses and riders within the confines of the outdoor arena where we had just been doing all that ground work. I hung in the saddle and managed a strong but futile attempt to pull the left rein so as to bend the horse away from his straight, irrepressible sprint.

"Let him go, Tom. Let him go," Harry Whitney's voice rang over a loudspeaker. The clinician's words pierced their way into the split-second rapid fire reflexes of thought synapsing in my brain just then. The taut left rein went slack as I reacted to The Voice in my head (Harry's voice that is...I know, it's scary). Niji ran,

Harry on Niji during the clinic in Hanover, Virginia.
(Pam Talley Stoneburner)

completely liberated from the annoyance of the leather tethers. I just concentrated on staying aboard, and recall sailing past another couple of surprised riders, and then noticing we were heading for the gate—the closed gate.

"Oh great!" I thought, and experienced an instant flashback.

Niji and I had been in this fix before. Five years earlier, we experienced just such a situation. (Yeah, five years later and I still haven't lost my touch to get Niji to run off with me and completely disrupt a clinic.) During that earlier clinic, complete with an outdoor arena packed full of horses and riders, he bolted. That time as we approached a fence, he stopped hard at the last second, the cinch broke, and the saddle with me still in it came off the horse, scooted along the ground, and I sailed clear out of the arena under the oak board fence between two posts.

This time I hung in the saddle, *and* the saddle hung on the horse. We stopped abruptly in a huff right at the gate.

"Rub him...now rub that horse!" The Voice in my head commanded.

I did. Then the adrenaline caught up and smacked me hard from behind making my heart beat in my throat, my fingers tingle, and my mouth go dry. Legs dangling as I sat there rubbing Niji like he was a good horse who'd just won the Derby, I realized my boots had come out of the stirrups somewhere along the way. Other than the trembling arms and mini tremors running through my body as the adrenaline continued to course through my veins, things with me were fine enough.

Niji heaved with each breath, nostrils flared, and looked around. I wondered just what he was feeling. I too looked around.

No one else had been sent asunder in the incident, for which I was very grateful.

Then the crazy part of the whole deal occurred to me. That Voice in my head that belonged to Harry...it kept telling me to do the completely counterintuitive thing. My horse bolts, so instead of pulling a rein to turn him to slow and stop, Harry says let him go. Run wild! Be free, you wacky horse! What was that about, anyway? I might just have to talk to This Voice in my head, I thought.

Then, on top of that, after Niji stopped, rather than putting him in time-out or revoking his driver's license for six months, there I was rubbing him in praise for nearly killing us. What was Harry seeing in this horse? Why did The Voice suggest I act this way in this situation?

This scenario stands out like an active volcano in the landscape of otherwise more typical peak and valley clinic experiences for me. Not really because it involved a furious volcanic type eruption with Niji's actions, but rather because Harry's advice at first seemed completely backwards. I didn't get into discussing it with him at that moment, and I can't really remember why not, but afterwards upon contemplation it became a perplexing riddle to me. That is what kept me reflecting on the moment frequently after it occurred. Why would he have said what he did, when he did?

The example provides a bold statement as to the kind of understanding Harry brings to light through his teaching. When I think about this event, even now, what stands out is how Harry's advice focused on the horse's feelings as the primary concern. I had adjusted things to gain a pretty good clamp on Niji's "misbehavior" for years. Most often I worked to stay ahead of it by keeping him "with me" mentally to the best of my ability at any given time. I redirected his thoughts sometimes away from trouble. Plus, I just finished all that working to break the grip of many thought magnets with him. Also, at home (and not in a particularly conscious effort), I developed an environment in which we rarely pushed up against anxiety in any serious mental way that could cause issues in the first place. I had learned what might get him close to a run off or melt down, and I went about removing those unpleasantries thinking it was improving the horse's deal.

In this latest bolting experience, I realized due to Harry's strange advice that I'd missed a big truth: that keeping a horse from blowing his lid by avoidance is not the same thing as diffusing from within the horse what causes that horse's to feel he needs to blow his lid.

There is no doubt that the clinic environment gave no cushy buffer zones like I had built up over time at home (even if it was done so unconsciously over time, thinking it was real improvement). Strange horses going in all directions with their humans, free horses roaming in paddocks just across the fence, new noises and smells—all this stuff pushed Niji and me clear out of our regular and predictable riding sphere. That wonderland at home was removed; you know, that place where horses rarely act up, not because they're going so well and just peachy with the world, but because the world is only allowed in to a certain degree.

It was quite an awakening when Niji proved to be so reactionary. I wanted (and thought I had made progress towards) a horse to ride out into the world. One to ride anywhere and to be dependable in real situations. However, it was clear even to me that work still needed to be done to get there with this horse. Even some basic goals at home remained to be achieved, like getting Niji to be a settled and regular mount for riding to other pastures over a couple of miles to feed other horses like I attempted when the trampoline factor reared its ugly head. But, such an explosion in the confines of an arena in the course of several days' hard clinic work came as a surprise, even after (perhaps especially after) all that hard won ground work progress. My previous efforts with Niji clearly in that moment were exposed to be far shorter of my goal than I would have guessed.

That gelding had not been through trouble with me in all of our experience together where I was able to support him and get to a better place from his perspective during a real problem. One might say, the horse lacked confidence in me as the rider, or he would not have felt the need to take control and run to the gate if he had. Another way to view it might be that I missed the trouble in my horse, and therefore when he was telling me all along he was in trouble, in his mind I ignored him until he couldn't take it any more and had to take control and run. Niji certainly didn't look to me for comfort and guidance when he felt overwhelmed, and trying for a one-rein-stop must not have been a helpful answer to my dilemma if Harry said to let the horse go.

In truth, as Harry said to let the reins go, I see now he knew the horse couldn't go but so far within the confines of that arena. Still, it seemed to me like there were a thousand acres for the runaway to gallop around in. The action perhaps was, I figured, in a sense saying to the horse, "okay...you're so bothered you need to have your head and go? Fine, go to it, it's okay." To continue to try and impose my will on that horse at that moment was not as productive as letting him follow through on what he felt he needed to do—for once.

It is also for certain, in retrospect, that Harry knew Niji would head for the gate and stop—that, for some reason, the gate would be his magic spot where his thoughts were projected, and when his body reached his thoughts there, he'd stop. Of course, I was not privy to this information at the time, but was just plain glad I stayed in the saddle.

Then, to follow up with rubbing Niji to sooth and comfort him at that moment, odd though it seemed, was the perfect timing to calm and support him when he really needed it. It helped to get him feeling better about things, including me, after being completely panicked.

Upon reflection of all this, the first point that comes to my mind about a bolting situation in general is that a person's instinctive reaction to a runaway horse is almost certainly to haul back on *both* reins. If someone is on a horse and holds a rein in each hand, and has no prior riding training, if that horse takes off suddenly, it's a pretty sure bet they are going to pull both reins equally to try and stop. That just seems to be innate human way to say, "Halt horse!"

Next, I realized my reaction to pull a single rein instead of both reins came from conditioning over time. I've listened to a chorus of clinicians sing the praises of the "one-rein-stop," and I've grown accustomed to disengaging the hind quarters as a fundamental maneuver for working with a horse. Even in controlled circumstances when riding, I often bend a horse around with a rein and spiral him down to a stop. It is a learned technique, and there are many reasons to use it at various times. In this particular scenario with Niji what matters is that my choice to grab a single rein was based on the often taught use of the exercise as a kind of emergency brake for horses.

The basic reasoning of the one-rein-stop is that if we bend the horse, the power of the hind quarters is brought somewhat off-line and therefore the energy sort of spills out to the side, so the horse is unable to continue as fast. Also, if applying pressure to one rein is successful in turning the horse, then the horse might be made to think around to the side rather than remaining mentally in full-forward-flight mode.

So, if all that one-rein stop stuff sounds so great, why did

Tom working Niji in the arena during the clinic in Hanover, Virginia where he bolted. (Terry McCoy)

Harry say to let the rein go? I asked Harry that question. Since he is clearly qualified to give the best answer, and what he said was the lesson I took from pondering and then discussing this ordeal, I'll leave it to Harry to explain.

"When he took off..." Harry said, "I don't know that the reason he took off was important, but when he took off his mind was gone. He was leaving. There was no question in his mind. So when you pulled on the rein it didn't affect him. He wasn't going to spiral around, or arc a circle, or anything. Why teach him that if you pull on the rein he can just run anyplace? So just release the rein and let him go! If he needs to go that bad, you might as well let him do it.

"If picking up the reins would have been able to bring him back and have him feel better, then he probably wouldn't have ended up in the position in the first place. So just let him go. You were in a fenced in space; where's he gonna go?

"If he'd have been out in a wide open space—if he could have run a ways—then you could have had a chance of bending him around. But, when he first blasted, his mind was so gone there was no chance, and besides that, you were in an arena with a bunch of other people. With his neck bent around he can't see where he's going as good as he could otherwise, and he'll run into somebody twice as quick than if he can stick his head out there where he's going and make plans. When they're running sideways with their neck bent, they'll crash you into the fence, slam into another horse...anything. You might as well just sit there and enjoy the ride!

"And then once they go a ways, they usually don't squirt very far, and then you can start to help them. Then they can hear it [the rein], but boy at first they can't. To me that's all the reasons I said, 'Let go.' He was determined on going and you weren't going to change it.

"The petting him afterwards is because—why did he take off?—because he was upset, scared, and worried. If you did anything that would cause him to think you were upset with him at that moment when he needed you, it would only add to his anxiety.

Harry watching the action in the outdoor arena at Mendin' Fences Farm in Tennessee with his wireless microphone draped around his neck and at the ready for commentary. (Tom Moates)

He didn't need to be in more trouble."

Niji and I got through that ordeal in pretty decent stride. Harry's words brought me back to reflect on how the horse's mind and his thought processes are the spot where we must work towards real and lasting improvement.

Harry differentiated between a horse being what I'd call "totally gone" mentally and "partially gone." Niji being totally gone when bolting was not reachable, period. No line of communication was going to get through a rein or anything else until he had a shift inside himself and felt safe enough to at least be open to conversation. Letting him move his feet and "squirt" a ways, that is with the rider doing nothing, or perhaps even supporting him with a little praise, allows the panicked moment to pass.

Then, when we get to where the horse is able to listen a little again, we can work with a rein, or halter rope, or whatever. The alternative (insisting on trying to control the horse during the panic) is not going to make the horse feel any better or want to be a partner with you. Rather, it is at least going to inflame the situation, if not cause a big wreck as he wrestles with his terrible trouble and you adding more to it.

We spent another couple days at that clinic with a goal of getting and keeping Niji's focus on me in both ground work and riding. His worry dissolved a bit, and his ability to stay with me greatly increased. It remained a lot of hard work, with him mentally leaving me and running around on the end of the line a fair bit. But it improved, and by the last day began to take less time and effort to sort out.

We went home to a whole new world in some ways. We rode

farther and did more in the saddle (safely and productively) than ever before. One of the biggest changes that has proven permanent around here with all horses is that I now go looking for what bothers Niji and the others rather than creating that buffered zone to work in where they are never pushed to a point that they want to bolt, mentally or physically. I seek out those troubling places, and then get right in there and work on them. That's a huge shift to my approach.

It seems to get the horses here more with-me and really dissolves some of their hang ups. When we venture out into the world, I hope it makes us better prepared to ride and do things, and those mental magnets no longer suck their brains out of there heads, and try to take their bodies with them away from me every five minutes.

Chapter 5

(Tom Moates)

Approaching a Horse Like a Windmill

The horse stood in the round pen with a halter and lead rope on, relaxed. The horse's owner handed off the rope to Harry. She'd asked the clinician to come in and see what he thought about the gelding.

The horse stood facing Harry, and the clinician stood there for a moment looking at the horse. A moment later, Harry walked towards him reaching one arm over his head and then the other as he went. Harry wore a pretty heavy nylon type of coat over a bunch of other layers since we were on an open mountain top in the Appalachians and the wind cut into us with a terrible chill at times. The scene made me think of a windmill with legs—one of those colossal slow ones in Holland with the flappy fabric rotors.

Such counterintuitive occurrences as this, I've learned, just seem to come with the territory around Harry.

I didn't recollect seeing this provoking move in his clinics before. Why, I wondered, watching these calisthenics from my plastic chair just beyond one of the round pen panels, move towards a horse in a manner that is potentially bothersome? There can be no other answer except to be potentially bothersome, I figured. Such a

Tom watches as Harry works a horse in the round pen in Hanover, Virginia. (Pam Talley Stoneburner)

provoking move is likewise a *thought* provoking move, and Harry must have wanted to see what the horse thought about an oncoming weird flappy human thing.

The lead rope in his hands, Harry advanced towards this horse (and a couple others over the week as well) like a windmill while at the same time putting enough feel on the line to keep both of the horse's eyes looking right a him. The equine reactions seemed predictable. Depending on the horse, they ranged from neck bracing, to the head flinging upwards and back, to a step or two backwards. These recoiling reactions lasted until Harry finally got to the horse and began rubbing the face, nose, and sometimes neck. Then, the horse relaxed some and seemed much relieved at the touch.

The simplicity of the maneuver (and at least its possible purpose), occurred to me pretty quickly. Especially since Harry did it to this first horse about a half dozen times in succession. Each time there was quite a bit of improvement, meaning the horse became more settled to his windmill approach.

The moral of this story is obviously to go out and antagonize your horse!

That's a little overstated, but not entirely out of the realm of truth. Harry might have done any number of things to check out how this horse was feeling. Maybe a hop, or spin the loose end of the lead rope over his head a little. Ultimately, as trust and confidence improve, the person ought to be able to do most anything around a horse with the horse remaining calm and relaxed. Really, Harry gave the horse a chance to be fine with his strange approach, although he knew the likely outcome.

I began to think this through: if we find a horse does not

react well to the windmill approach (substitute any potentially unsettling maneuver here like holding a plastic dewormer syringe or bottle of water when walking up to the horse, or skipping to your horse, etc.), then we have two options...well three if you consider not doing anything at all an option. One is to try and protect the horse from ever experiencing the action so he never has to be made nervous or unsettled. Or two, work it through and get him feeling better about the thing so it melts away.

Note that the windmill is just a random deal Harry hit on to use sometimes, and not something he does with every horse. I often feel the need to clearly articulate this point when I describe what I've witnessed in his clinics because there is a tendency to try and make the work of clinicians into A, B, C, type programs—on both the part of many teachers and students. I understand the desire to try and simplify a way to get better with horses and to try and get that information accessible to everybody, but every horse is different and I'm sure Harry would want it made clear that there is nothing standardized to his approach. The lessons he works to impart seek to cause more of a shift in consciousness in the person, trying to get them to ask certain questions, notice how to better read what is going on in the horse, and then work at bettering the horse's situation through their own creative means.

So, the windmill (which is just my silly name for it) is not a step of some program to test every horse. It wouldn't matter if you did try it on every horse you worked with, but the point here is that it is just an example of one way to be a bit creative around a horse to begin to see what the horse is thinking. If you explore a little here and there with your horse to see how he thinks and reacts to a few unusual moves on your part, then a picture should start to develop, if you pay attention, of how settled and with-you the horse is.

I bet Harry rarely sees a horse in a clinic that would be okay with the windmill. Some horses are more skitterish by nature than others, of course. Any kind of horse, however, might take a person's odd or energetic approach more in stride if we would seek to help them be okay with that sort of thing from time to time. It made me think we'd do our horses a heap of good if we'd fiddle with finding and working on such little things consistently. Not to mention the fact that by finding and fixing these little things, we also really are working on big things, just before they ever get the chance to be big!

Flagging a horse can fall right into this same category. I've always been intrigued by how easily a horse is able to discern between when a flag is just flapping around meaninglessly or when it is charged with the feel from a person to ask the horse to do something.

Harry on Jubal with a flag at the ready in Floyd, Virginia. (Tom Moates)

The flag must be in the hands of someone who is handy enough to provide the intended difference clearly, otherwise confusion sets in and make things quite unsettling for the horse. The other thing that always amazed me about the flag, and the exact same is true here with the windmill maneuver, is how the horse can be incredibly apprehensive of the moving flappy object near to him—just jumping out of his skin sometimes—until it touches him. Once contact is made, he settles into it. It seems to reason that strange things near a horse would be even more troubling if they touched him. But, the opposite proves true. The typical horse is far more worried about something close but unfelt, and much relieved when he can feel it and begin to use the sense of touch to help understand what is going on.

The crowd sits behind a truck and trailer for a windbreak in Floyd, Virginia, watching the action in the round pen—left to right: Loletta Rogers, Kathy Baker, Eden Bowen, Arika Legg, Jake Legg, and Carol Moates. (Tom Moates)

Another aspect of the windmill deal, I guessed leaning back in my chair, is that the horse ought to pay attention to you when you're in the neighborhood. An exercise like reaching your arms over your head can be a means to say, "Hey...I'm right here in front of you. Focus here on me, buddy." That relates to Jubal, me, and the big tree; the sorrel's thoughts were over somewhere else, I wasn't getting through to him, and right smack in front of him was a big tree that we nearly smashed into. A horse might stand there in the round corral and sort of look at you, but not really. He might be somewhere else mentally, maybe looking past you. A sudden or strange movement might snap his focus on you, or at least test to see where his thoughts are at the moment and whether or not you are of any significance to the horse. It seemed to me this horse, although facing Harry, had not been really focused on him. The arms over his head deal sure made Harry more important to the horse.

The windmill speaks volumes about how simple it is to inquire as to how a horse is feeling about a few things. Harry is always keeping an eye out for spots in a horse where things aren't right—where there's a worry, a stiffness, an imbalance—these he shares aloud during clinics. He's incredibly good at seeing things I never would have noticed. The windmill approach, however, drove home a few points and since have helped me to keep them in the forefront of my horse work. Namely, to keep searching for little sticky troubles with a horse rather than trying to avoid them, and that the most simple actions around a horse provide big insights if one pays attention to the horse.

Watching Harry do the windmill stunned me a little at first. Just think about seeing a guy standing there with someone's perfectly happy calm horse, and then just out of nowhere he goes: flap, flap, flap!

"Yikes! Crazy person!" says the horse.

It is a bit startling. The strange moment was great though, because there was no mistaking what just happened. It was obvious.

Go ahead and walk up to almost any horse like that and see what happens. Yep, the neck braces, the head flies up, the horse backs up. Yet, we spend tons of time around our horses heads with lead ropes, halters, hands, bridles, brushes—all kinds of stuff and many different movements. I know the horse in that round pen with Harry that day was no different that most other frequently ridden horses at an average clinic, or anywhere else. So, why then was that little spot that really bothered this horse (and no doubt tons of others) never noticed before? Or if noticed, why haven't we paid attention and got it smoothed out for them? Five minutes was all it took to start getting the horse in the round pen a whole bunch better about it.

I'm convinced from watching Harry, and then playing with my horses too, that we humans are just oblivious sometimes. It took quite awhile for me to change my demeanor from tip toeing around horses to being assertive and actually picking around to find the little spots that are troubling to the horse. Now I like to know what they are, and I like to get them worked out of the horse before they become the primer charge for a much bigger blast, and maybe a nasty wreck.

Jubal provided me a perfect example of this one day, and it really caught me of guard. But that's a whole other story...so I'll devote the next chapter to it.

Chapter 6

(Kathy Baker)

POSTED!
(Riding Jubal on the Job)

In October each year, a great job to do with the help of a saddle horse jumps to my mind. Hunting season is just about to start and I like to get around the boundary of our property and check the posted signs. Many of the yellow Tyvek "No Trespassing" signs that mark the perimeter of our land will be missing, or flapping in the breeze half stapled to trees and fence posts. I like to get a staple gun and new roll of signs and get the yellow beacons all tacked up. It helps (I hope) avoid armed trespassers stumbling onto the land and into our horse pastures during hunting season.

The terrain is pretty rough along much of the fence line, with some steep rocky mountain sides to negotiate. The rest of the route is varying degrees of overgrown pasture, trees, brush, tangled masses of multifloral rose, thickets of mountain laurel, and deer trails. It is a long, tough hike on foot. There's no chance of getting a vehicle around most of it. It is, however, fairly well suited for a sure footed horse.

In truth, I've tried for years unsuccessfully to get this mission accomplished horseback. I'd set out in the saddle with visions of walking easily along the fence looking ahead for any misfit signs. I saw myself riding up along side any of them hanging partially loose. In my mind I leaned over from the saddle and tacked them back in place with the staple gun, then easily rode on to continue the task.

It never happened that way.

Many jobs went pretty well with these same horses during that time, even when out on the farm in some unusual places, but the posted sign check never did. Perhaps the density of the overgrowth in many areas made the surroundings more worrisome than the others? Regardless of the reasons (I could conger up quite a few more), I inevitably ended up a pedestrian with the added burden of leading the horse most of the way. Of course I took the opportunity while out there in the middle of nowhere to do more ground work and see about sorting through some of the trouble—just what I wasn't looking for at the time. In terms of getting the job done horseback, though, my hopes sank. My thousand pound companion's job altered slightly from carrying me, to merely helping pack around a five ounce roll of paper-thin signs and a one pound staple gun.

Now, however, for the first time I had Jubal the wonder horse. And we were freshly back from a week of horsemanship Bible clinic with Harry and Ronnie Moyer that Carol and I hosted up here in Virginia. Ronnie and Harry partnered up quite a few years ago and started putting together these unique Christian clinics. Several times each year they arrange their spiraling schedules to overlap in a few places and offer them.

Ronnie is a cowboy chaplain from Simla, Colorado who works tirelessly with his wife, Becky, in their ministry (www.livingspringranch.org). He is also very active in rodeo, and bull fighting is one of his many talents (which I know for certain takes a lot of faith!). In general, Harry teaches the horsemanship part and Ronnie gives scriptural instruction. The two, however, overlap quite seamlessly. The fellowship is astonishing among the groups I've been to, and the horses never fail to provide inspiration for Biblical and horsemanship study.

I felt a whole new confidence to get the posted sign check done this time.

Jubal had proven himself an increasingly solid citizen in the months of work we'd done leading up to the time for this task. I can only hope he was thinking the same of me. The recent clinic proved a big leap forward in an already very decent relationship. Riding out and getting a job done continued to improve. Much of what I took to be his old ranch horse demeanor seemed to be back after getting past some of the initial trouble that traveled with him from being ridden by an inexperienced rider cross country, discussed earlier. Plus, he was shod, which clearly helped avoid the ouchiness the barefoot horses experienced on many of the rocky surfaces

Ronnie Moyer showing one of his many talents–bull fighting. (Moyer Ministries Collection)

around here. Jubal and I rode everywhere these days—on the county roads, among cattle, around neighbors' pastures where I'd never been before, and along all kinds of fences with my neighbor, Derrick Hicks, and his horse, Rose. We'd ridden along the river that borders our property and over many gravel roads. I felt renewed confidence that the big sorrel and I were going to get this sign checking job done this year properly, finally!

To my great surprise, we nearly didn't make it past the saddling phase.

I got Jubal out of his pasture. I brushed him, saddled him, and picked his feet. A halter was on him at this point, with the lead rope tied to a fence post. I put a handful of new signs into my jacket pocket from the truck. I found the shiny metal staple gun and a packet of staples under the seat, and made sure it was fully loaded. I thought about the best way to carry it on the trail, and decided to tie a string onto the handle so I could loop it over the saddle horn to hang. Then I closed the truck door and went towards Jubal to get started.

Just to recap, and show my mindset in that moment: here's a horse who was one of a pair that alternated between carrying a full pack saddle rig and a saddle with a rider, from the Canadian border at North Dakota to the Mexican border at El Paso, Texas. I can't imagine all the stuff that must have been tied to this horse every day for months on end. It never occurred to me that a staple gun might pose a problem. Heck, by now I'd flagged him plenty of times without any outrageous reactions.

I walked right up to his mid section with the staple gun and went to hang it on the saddle horn. Before it touched the leather, Jubal panicked. The big gelding took off backwards nearly taking the fence with him. Luckily, the staple gun remained in my hand (not hooked onto the horse flapping around like a metallic cheetah latched to his withers), and my horsemanship reflexes instantly moved the offending object away from him. Lucky too, that while Jubal gave the lead rope a horrendous yank for a second which pulled the fence post over quite a bit, he just as quickly yielded to the pressure and stepped forward as I backed up. We both stood there then, just looking at each other.

If any concern had existed in me that some object might trouble Jubal, you bet I'd have introduced it a lot more carefully. I set the staple gun on the tailgate of the truck, then went over and untied Jubal from the fence post. I gave him plenty of length on the lead rope and I walked back over and picked up the staple gun. He paid close attention to it, and kept all the distance he could. I moved the handle just a little, which made a slight metallic click which sent Jubal over the edge and he pulled against the line to flee. Hmmm, I thought, this is a really big reaction...I wonder what might have caused this?

Of course, the cause really doesn't matter. What a person does now in the middle of such a problem is what matters. Horse trouble presents itself on its own terms, and it is up to us to work with what we're given. I knew all about presenting spooky things to horses by this point in my experience. I just treated the staple gun like I would any such troubling object, like a flag, bag, or fly spray bottle.

The lead rope in one hand and staple gun in the other I asked Jubal to walk towards me. I figured if the horse moves towards the spooky thing it helps his confidence a little, rather than me moving towards him, which could seem more like it was chasing him and might amplify his worry. Many times I'd seen Harry present the flag to a horse for the first time by bringing it right straight forward to his nose at nose level. The comment he made in doing so was that when horses are loose and check out some strange curiosity on their own, that this is the preferred method—to touch it (and no doubt smell it as well) with the nose. Then work to rub the horse with it, maybe on either side of the face, eventually getting down the neck and to the body.

This went about like I expected once I realized how terrified Jubal was of the staple gun. He was tense and dubious of it at first, but after five minutes of getting him used to it and feeling it on him he settled down. Then I tried the same thing while making a slight

Stoney, left, and Jubal, right, enjoy turn out time at the clinic in Floyd, Virginia. (Tom Moates)

click with the handle, and we started all over again. The noise was an added element of trouble to Jubal, but the process went about the same. Finally, I got it hanging on the saddle horn and was able to bounce it around up there without him tensing up. So I saddled up and headed up the road to start the task.

It went great! The riding part, anyway. What I'd been unable to achieve in previous years on other horses finally came through on Jubal. He was a little fidgety at first. I just kept riding a line with our mission in mind, checked in with him pretty often by tipping his head with a rein, backing, or making a circle as we went along. When

Ronnie works with Woody, Eden Bowen's Chincoteague pony, in Floyd, Virginia. (Tom Moates)

a sign needed stapling, I dismounted and used care to take down the staple gun. Then I held a rein while stapling and went through the task of reintroducing the tool to Jubal before hanging it back on the saddle and remounting. We spent a couple hours that afternoon on the job, and things improved as we went along. I came home with a big smile on my face.

The next two days we went out again getting to new stretches of the property boundary. It surprised me a little how skittish he was of the staple gun again each time we started. I did the flagging exercise with it before saddling each time. Jubal did show less trouble each day in that respect, although I could see his concern wasn't completely eliminated.

The really awesome aspect of this experience was how well we got along in the riding. Between the work we'd done together including the recent clinic, having the focus of a job, being absorbed in sorting out the stable gun issue, and Jubal being just plain awesome, there was never a substantial problem with the riding. The riding became so matter-of-fact that there was no trouble with Jubal staying with me as we went along through the varying terrain.

The staple gun episode, though, remains fresh in my mind as a critical lesson. It's important not to make assumptions about what may or may not produce an unforeseen reaction in a horse. Jubal could have hurt himself, or me, and in another situation any number of bad things could have resulted from the staple gun scare. I'm more vigilant now not to take what other people tell me is certain truth about a horse if I haven't seen it myself—like, "Oh this horse has ridden across America, he's ready to pack anything anywhere." Or to make such assumptions myself. The staple gun incident seems to pop to mind every time I have something in my hand my own horses may be unfamiliar with. There is much to be said on this point, and it is important enough that I want to cover a little more about it in the next chapter.

Chapter 7

(Terry McCoy)

People's Perceptions, Advice, and Other Wild Goose Chases.

Knowing something of an unfamiliar horse's history may prove helpful in some ways. However, when it comes time to get down to business with a newcomer it is best to get your information "straight from the horse's mouth." The experience of getting familiar with Festus and Jubal drove home that really important point.

These two Quarter Horses in no way lacked saddle experience, as mentioned in the Introduction. First, they began life as working ranch horses. Then, traveling border to border across America's roadways provided them a range of experiences under saddle like few horses get exposed to in this modern era.

During the course of acquiring the geldings, it was mentioned to me several times by various horse folk along the way that since they had just completed such a big journey, they should be perfectly seasoned road ready veterans. Obviously, they assumed, since the horses made such a long trip, they must be ready for anything. Just hop on and hit the trail.

It stands to reason, I suppose, that if some fellow gets two horses and makes a successful fifteen hundred mile journey over five months, it ought to be true. But, in other walks of life I have seen so many horses considered to be "dead broke" that I wouldn't throw a leg over, that honestly I assumed a dubious position here as well. Still, I had hopes high enough for these two horses that I went forward with bringing them here to Virginia.

By the time this all happened, the view that horses are vehicles that can be trained just to react to mechanical aids and cues that simply should respond the same to any rider was ancient history in my mind. Harry helped wreck that for me. When approaching a new horse now, my gaze instinctively probes to see how he feels. In an eye-blink, my mind switches to figuring where things need improving first, and how I might go about getting the horse better off. When I got Festus and Jubal home, I began to take in what I could understand of their condition, and began to see what I could do to get us all moving in the direction I wanted.

On the other hand, just for the record, there can be the opposite dilemma. Like when Jubal came back after Harry used him at Mendin' Fences Farm in Tennessee as a saddle horse for seven weeks recently—if the horse is in better shape than I am, it puts me

Harry and Ronnie watch Tom as he rides Jubal in Floyd, Virginia. (Terry McCoy)

in the awkward position of trying hard to up my game to meet the horse's refined state and not bring him back down to my level too quickly.

Looking back, I feel lucky to have had a "let's wait and see what I've got" stance with Festus and Jubal and not to have been swept up in a tide of unrealistic expectations. I know in the past, I'd have easily fallen into that trap. It wouldn't have changed where the horses were mentally and physically, but going through the sharp adjustment of opening my eyes to reality would have been all the more unpleasant.

I often see folks with horses completely unsuited to their abilities. It is a very disagreeable situation to observe. I hate seeing a horse jigging all around, neck braced, head up, wide eyed with a rider clamping down on the reins and barely keeping the horse in check... but it is not uncommon. Less outwardly visible but equally troubling scenarios, where the horse's mind is not with the rider and there is a crookedness and lack of responsiveness in the horse, is more typical than not among the riders I see (and I will include myself in this category, so don't think I'm too delusional). Even though I was on the lookout for trouble with the two new geldings, some expectations clearly existed in my mind. This became evident when I felt some shock for just how unfit for use the Big-Uns were when they arrived.

Jubal and Festus came to the mountains of Virginia from sunny south Texas in the cold dead of February. I turned them out to pasture and just allowed them a few weeks to eat and recuperate. Feeding and checking on them a couple of times each day provided the opportunity for us to get acquainted.

Right away Festus, who sported a black coat with brown

muzzle and lower legs (in my mind giving the impression of a mule's markings), showed quite a bit of worry. I'd call it "skitterishness," because the apprehension included the tendency to move away from me, and when loose in the pasture he proved pretty tricky to get a hand on. He expressed his feelings outwardly. It was plain to see trepidation in his eye and a quick flight response to any sudden movement.

Jubal, the bigger, rounder, sorrel horse, was more stoic. I figured at the time that he could be a horse that stuffed things, and that it might become evident how he really felt all at once—but I

Harry showing the group a few rope tricks on Jubal between riders during a clinic in Tennessee. (Tom Moates)

wasn't certain about this. Jubal sported a freeze brand on his right thigh, a big "TM," which seems rather cryptic since my name is Tom Moates. What are the odds of that?

Perhaps the most surprising initial discovery was that these horses both were terrified of ropes. Jubal, I know for sure, had been a roping horse. Both, obviously, had packed a ton of gear and so lived constantly around ropes and straps and all kinds of stuff. Yet, when I went to do a little ground work with either one at first, they flat bolted when I'd introduced the tail of the halter rope to them in most any way. Especially if I just tried to toss the end of the rope onto their backs or butts, they panicked so hard it was all I could do to keep a grip on the halter rope and bend them back around to face me and stop. Even when circling them around me on a lead, if I went in to touch a shoulder with a handful of the rope's tail, they'd flee from it and get bug eyed. How odd, I thought.

The lesson was most pronounced when I went to ride Jubal. Festus had the knee injury, so other than just giving a couple short test rides, I elected to leave him to heal for many months as the vet suggested.

Jubal apparently was conditioned to going forward in a big way. He'd stand for me to get a foot in the first stirrup, but before the other leg was over his back he already was heading down the path at a robust walk. That reflex was the first thing I addressed with him. I expect he was accustomed to getting his day going as fast as possible so it could be over with, since he spent each day of his long journey traveling somewhere new which only ended after around twenty miles or more were covered. Stopping likewise was hardly in his vocabulary. Mentally, he was a thousand miles away from me when I went to do anything with him. I started working on these things to the best of my ability at that time, on the ground and from the saddle. The challenge was formidable. The task to get Jubal with me and feeling okay about pretty basic stuff took quite a bit of effort, especially at first. The big gelding would take off in flight from a flag or rope, yank on the line, and even initial progress took some days to take hold.

Through a gate from where these geldings were kept was a fifty acre pasture with steep hills and about thirty head of cattle. It seemed a great place for a real test ride. I wanted to try Jubal out in a setting away from his home turf and get him away from Festus to see how things went. Plus I figured it ought to provide an idea of what this former ranch horse thought about cattle these days. And, to tell the truth, I was dying to have a good basic trail ride without a mental meltdown.

The big sorrel led through the gate fine. I mounted and rode Jubal about fifty feet away heading towards some cows in the distance on a hill when I started to feel it. The horse began to get that nervous fluttery feeling under me. Keeping him with me and lined out in the direction I wanted to travel quickly became increasingly difficult. Within a few strides he was completely crooked. His brain went behind us back to the other pasture, and I had a job on my hands working my legs and the reins trying to keep him moving where I hoped to go.

Festus, who was left behind, never called out to Jubal; the horse just kept on grazing and seemed to care less that we'd left the scene. Jubal, however, was falling to pieces at a quick pace. I used everything I had at my disposal at that time to get his mind with me, but it was no use. I got down and tried some ground work. I remounted, rode circles, and disengaged the hind end many times. Things got progressively worse. I did make it over near the cows riding the twisted up mess under me to the best of my ability. For safety's sake, however, I finally gave it up and walked the horse back to his pasture. I figured my best bet was to quit and live to work on this pretty severe herd bound behavior another day.

This example, like the staple gun incident that happened much later, seems like a great one to show the dangers of making assumptions about a horse yourself, or taking the advice of others regarding horses you don't know. Even when I was being cautious about my initial preconceived notions with Festus and Jubal, things

Kathy Baker works with Ari in the round pen at Mendin' Fences Farm as Harry and others look on. (Tom Moates)

were much worse at first than I would have guessed. The sharp reactions to ropes and Jubal's separation anxiety, for example, could have gotten me in a wreck if I hadn't taken time to explore where these horses were, and done so in a place where it was relatively safe to do so.

On the other hand, Harry brought up a really good point when we discussed this topic. He reminded me of an incident with Carol's leopard Appaloosa, Stoney, where I got bucked off during a clinic in Virginia (don't worry, all the details of this wreck are in an upcoming chapter). That horse surprised Carol, Harry, and me with his actions. Given my previous experience with that gelding over a couple of years, Harry pointed out that I likely would have given someone else a wrong report on his current mindset that day.

If I had brought Stoney to the clinic for someone else to ride, for example, which easily could have happened, I certainly would have explained what a safe mount he was. In retrospect, we know what a mistaken assumption that would have been for that horse at that particular time. So this idea of being wary of people's perceptions and advice runs in both directions.

Horses, like people, are living creatures with good days and bad days. Both of us bring to the table our past experiences along with taking in what is happening at the moment. Now I try harder to make a point to see what the horse is telling me himself, whether it be a horse I know well or one I have never seen before. Of course a horse's past is of interest, and provides some clues to what is there to be worked with. I don't mean to simply ignore information like past injuries or tendencies that are known about a horse. Go ahead and glean some important insights from others who have known a horse.

The main information that needs focus, however, is what the horse tells us. We do well to pay attention and to try and avoid making decisions based on hearsay, or falling into the trap of giving too much of it ourselves.

Chapter 8

(Tom Moates)

Another Piece of the Puzzle

"If I firm up a little, I'd want my horse to get *more attentive* rather than flee," Harry said.

In that moment I saw clearly the difference between a horse reflexively fleeing when being asked something by the human, or taking the feel of a person's request as a welcomed cue to see what he should do next. It proved another profound piece of the horsemanship puzzle for me.

The black colt in the round pen with Harry belonged to Suzy FitzSimmons. She'd hauled him with a couple other older horses from Minnesota down to Mendin' Fences Farm in Tennessee for a few weeks of clinics. Mendin' Fences (www.mendinfencesfarm.com) is owned by Linda Bertani and Vic Thomas, and hosts Harry every year. The gelding, named Eddie, being a warmblood, already was the size of a mature horse of other familiar breeds, but at only eighteen months old he was the youngest horse I'd ever seen Harry work up to that time.

Suzy FitzSimmons leads her colt, Eddie, for a session in the round pen in Tennessee. (Tom Moates)

"I thought he was a pretty big example," Harry shared with me later when we discussed what I'd taken from that session. "It just hit me the way he was fleeing that if you firm up any to try and get him more attentive, it just tipped him over the edge. It didn't bring his attention to you, it just sent him away."

The idea Harry teaches to get a horse's thought with you and then use the weightless thought to have the horse move himself, had been pretty clear to me for some years. This "with-you-ness" of Harry's I clearly perceive to be in contrast to horses being driven to move, even when such examples are presented as "pressure and release." This new example I witnessed, though, had me seeing a new angle on Harry's teaching.

Certainly, when working with a horse's thought, having the horse's attention is essential. So often my horses' minds drift elsewhere and it becomes necessary to actively bring them back to me mentally before moving forward and getting something accomplished. I take responsibility for not being important enough to them for them to stay with me sometimes. Also, for not providing the handling to have it better sorted out by now, even though I'm getting better at seeing and dealing with it.

Checking in with a little feel on the lead rope or a rein to see if the horse is really present in mind has become quite regular for me. I expect Harry knows where the horse is mentally much more intuitively than I do, but I need a pretty obvious method to tell the difference. If the horse's mind is elsewhere, and I don't get a quick soft response to my requests, then I must somehow say, "Hey! Wake up! We've got a job to do!" before the horse says, "Oh...right, hey there...what's that you want?" My move to get his attention then is along the lines of flipping the lead rope, backing the horse, kicking some dirt, or slapping a chap.

The new observation and statement from Harry regarding the colt in the round pen had me realizing that there is another layer to this work that I hadn't seen clearly before. That a person should build into a horse the tendency to produce a welcoming response to *any* deliberate focus or bit of firmness from the human rather than allowing an initial bit of flight response to get established in there. This notion was subtle enough that I hadn't fully captured it.

In other words, it can be that the human picks up the lead rope to prepare to ask the horse something and the horse mentally flees, sidesteps, tunes out, or otherwise says, "Oh bother," like Winnie the Pooh—so the person first must get the horse's attention before moving on (hopefully) in a situation of with-you-ness. Or, on the other hand, as Harry was explaining, the response to just firming up on the lead rope can be a horse's instantaneous attention and a genuine preparation in the body and mind for any request that might come next from the human. It's a contented, relaxed, welcomed reaction from the horse to firmness from the person. The person firms up and the horse feels good about it. These represent two very different scenarios, even though they may both eventually lead to the horse being with you.

"When a horse is concerned, or his mind is gone, when you firm up there's a waiting till he checks in to see what's wanted," Harry explained. "Most people just try to get the action out of him, they don't worry about him coming back and checking in to be okay with the human, they just want this physical action."

I watched Harry get a little firm on the colt's lead rope and saw the horse first throw his head up a bit and clearly show that his eyes and thought were fleeing in the opposite direction. Harry kept up the firmness on the line. He didn't escalate, but he did hold out and maintain his intensity. The clinician just sustained the firmness until the colt brought his thought to Harry and relaxed into that moment a little, then released. It took a little while at first. I wondered about how well I'd be able to stick it out and get a change,

Eden Bowen bridles her Chincoteague pony, Woody, at a clinic in Floyd, Virginia. (Terry McCoy)

and if I could see the change at the right moment if it was me in the round pen. The changes in the colt laid the groundwork for what Harry wanted to build into the horse's make-up. After just a little while in the round pen, the colt started to flee less to requests and showed substantial attention and comfort when Harry firmed up and began to ask something of him. It refined to the point that with a little intention on the line, it was easy to see the colt instantly look right at Harry to see what he wanted next.

"You can firm up and get a horse to leap into a canter," Harry said as another example in our later conversation, "but he might be more mentally gone than before you asked for the transition.

Harry directs a horse's thought in the round pen in Tennessee. (Tom Moates)

But, I'd like to think that if I had to firm up just a little because he wasn't there [mentally]—instead of fleeing into the transition, he got mentally attentive and heard what it was I was asking. And there is a difference in that.

"Sometimes people are leading a horse, and the horse goes to pass them, so they wiggle their lead rope, they flip it, they do something to slow him down—but what I so often see is he squints his eyes, throws his head up, and slows down to avoid the pressure, but he's still looking past them thinking about hurrying on. There's no change in the mental. He hasn't come back and got more attentive to what they want. They just got in the way of his movement. And, so, that actually will build in where the horse gets where he can tolerate it—some pressure, some firmness, something from the human—and still hang on to this other thought. Instead of building in that, he needs to let go of that and get more attentive to what's wanted."

In Tennessee that week at a table talk after lunch, Harry discussed how if people handle firmness correctly, it provides the opportunity for the horse to feel good about the firmness before there ever is a release to it because he *knows* a moment of clarity is at hand. Consistent clarity over time builds constant confidence in an outcome, even in the moments before it happens if set up right.

If the human handles firmness consistently, always using it as a precursor to asking something specific of the horse and providing a release timed to build in the horse's attention, relaxation, and understanding, then there is every reason for the horse to consider firmness a very positive experience. This can ingrain in the horse so there comes a time when, for example, a person is riding and there is a need to do something quickly, so he grabs the reins and the horse is right there to follow along and go where he needs to go without bracing or fighting against it. But, it also builds a complete with-you-ness where even if nothing is going on and you pick up the reins quietly, the horse responds immediately and looks to see if the rider will ask anything next. The whole spectrum of experience is covered this way if we get it right with the horse.

The firmness discussed here, however, must not come from a negative attitude.

"When do most people firm up?" Harry asked me.

I paused thinking about it.

"When they want to cause trouble for the horse, really," he said. "They're mad at him. They're trying to punish him. He's in trouble somehow. He gets in trouble, maybe not even understanding why he was in trouble. It's like, you can scream and yell at a kid, tell him how stupid he is—that doesn't mean he understands what he did wrong. But you can firm up, speak rather firm and cross to a child and explain the importance of why he shouldn't have been doing what he was doing, and why it's important to do this other thing, and it has meaning. Later, he goes to get a little lost in that area, and all you've got to do is clear your throat. He doesn't panic, he doesn't start crying and run for cover because he's gonna get killed; his whole mindset just changes. And it's the same way with the horse.

"You can either put trouble in that for the horse, where he feels like he was in trouble, or you can bring a clarity that will actually get him more attentive. So then when he goes to get lost in some area, all you have to do is firm up a little and he comes back and checks in. Then he's available, you can direct him to come out better."

Thinking about this now I realize from experience that the opposite, namely that each time I'm not firm enough, likewise can add trouble to the horse. Wishy-washy handling is confusing and can cause the horse to flounder around simply from lack of understanding of what is expected of him. He won't feel confident about a lack of firmness in the human, and therefore won't readily feel good about the situation. This sets him up to want to take his thoughts elsewhere to a place where he thinks he is better off and more in control of his situation.

Since then, I've enjoyed doing some simple ground work to see what reaction occurs when I firm up on the lead rope. Like with Harry and the colt in the round pen that day, I want to start paying more attention to how the horse feels about it when he comes around and concentrates on me. Instead of the bigger reactions I have used to break loose a horse's lack of attention, I'm working to be ahead of that situation. I've tried to reduce the need for using the kind of big attention getters that often cause an initial head tossing or other fleeing response before the attention comes in. Instead, I'm spending time playing with firmness of various degrees to see if I can build up to where that firmness equals comfort and concentration in my horses.

Now I've seen in Harry's work that when done right, this provides a chance for the horse to actually embrace firmness from the person. This can happen even ahead of a release since he can bet on a clear request coming next if handled right. This piece of the puzzle was a long time coming to my attention. But, its subtle difference in my eyes is likely not so subtle for the horse.

Fleeing or being drawn by comfort are opposites. A horse's head flinging upwards and away represents a completely different feeling in the horse than lowering the head, looking at the person, and licking his lips. Even slight variations of these opposites can be indicators of much larger icebergs below the surface in the horse. It is this kind of awareness which auditing a clinic fosters since such close observation is possible.

Chapter 9

(Tom Moates)

So Simple

"So simple, yet so complex," I thought. Harry was riding a horse and getting a ton done with him. I gazed on, soaking it all in.

I stood leaning on a metal fence panel at one end of the arena at Mendin' Fences Farm in Tennessee and watched. Harry rode a Morgan named, Heyson, owned by Catherine Millard from Georgia. The gelding sported a rather long and curly mane and tail, and was black except for a white right hind foot and a little snip visible when the thick forelock blew to the side. It was Thursday afternoon in a Monday through Friday clinic, and a group ride was going on. What unfolded there with the Morgan was a kind of work I had witnessed Harry do several times before. Harry got through to this horse by riding him, and he made quite a positive change in less than an hour.

By contrast, in clinics Harry often works horses in the round pen—either from another horse, on foot, or coaches someone else who is working a horse. Often in those instances, one or two troubles get singled out and focused on. Such sticky points get the clinician's attention because the horse owner notices certain troubles and wants help getting them sorted out. A whole range of additional horsemanship stuff may surface at these times too, but they still tend to follow along a rather narrow path relating to a particular concern.

The instance with the Morgan represents a somewhat different approach, I thought, standing there watching intently. When Harry gets on a horse and rides, especially with some room like in an arena, a wider spectrum of experience occurs between the horse and him. Many times it is prompted by an owner saying, "Harry, ride my horse!" which means just that—no specific problem to work on right then, "Just ride him and see what you think." This kind of ride is a full contact sport, and you've got to be quick to observe even some of what is going on between the horse and Harry.

Perhaps it is not entirely accurate to differentiate between what I witnessed with the Morgan and much of the other work Harry does in clinics. I do see him ride a horse in much the same way in the "more narrowly focused" instances too. Maybe it is all the same thing, but right then it seemed to me that there is a difference. Perhaps the distinction is more in the fact that sometimes, like with the Morgan, Harry takes off and starts working a horse wide open with his own agenda? Or maybe he's free styling? He just goes for it. It becomes a magnificent example of what this clinician is able to accomplish when it's just the horse and him without the confines of a specific problem, like being bad to saddle or hard to ride to the left.

The distinction I seek to explain (I think), is that while Harry works a horse just as well all the time, sometimes he breaks it down. That makes it easier for others to catch certain parts of what he is doing. Occasionally, though, he lets loose and enjoys the opportunity to just work a horse wide open to the best of his abilities without compartmentalizing and demonstrating clearly smaller aspects of the whole. It must be a personal joy to him since it flows with a rhythm I don't notice at the times when the nuts and bolts of horsemanship are demonstrated more individually. A ride like this one unfolds, moment by moment. I feel like I'm watching Michelangelo painting a masterpiece—the master is in the zone and the paint, brushes, canvas, and blobs of color are speaking to him as much as he's guiding them into inspired forms. Harry likewise guides the horse-blob into a more inspired form. It provides a chance for folks like me to witness what that kind of unhindered talent and proficiency looks like. It's a goal to work towards.

I remember saying to Harry as he rode that I bet I could write a chart to show what had unfolded between him and that horse, yet when I go to work a horse, I can't always access and produce that kind of seriously helpful scenario. I said I wish I could "own" the knowledge to do what he was doing just then—that I could have it right there to offer a horse whenever the opportunity arises.

Harry said something like, "You mean get it in your bones?"

"Yes...exactly."

I'll not be able to convey nearly what took place between the Morgan and Harry in words here. However, I wish to try because I saw so much unfold in a single ride. Having seen this kind of

Catherine Millard lopes her horse, Heyson, in the round pen at Mendin' Fences Farm. (Tom Moates)

situation before with Harry and other horses in years past, I want to see if some important points might get onto the page if I share what I witnessed with Harry and that sweaty Morgan on a hot May afternoon in Tennessee.

The owner had been riding the horse for a half hour in the round pen next to the arena working on transitioning up through the trot to the lope and back down. The horse penned his ears when going in to the lope. He didn't act up, but the ears seemed a window into his mind regarding how he felt about loping. It was after working on that with some progress that she came back into the arena and asked Harry to ride the horse.

Harry mounted and got maybe three steps into the ride before he started backing the Morgan pretty abruptly. The backing served a barrage of purposes. First, the horse's mind already had left the scene that quickly, and Harry was saying, "Hello, I'm up here and you've got the stay with me."

That mental inflexibility likewise manifested as a dullness (unresponsiveness, or hardness) on the reins. Harry put enough pressure on the reins to get the horse backing and then continued the request until he felt a hint of softening in the horse, then released. He'd ask to go forward, but any time the horse would step off without relaxing into it (which was all the time at first) Harry backed him. After hanging in there with the Morgan for quite awhile, a change began to come through. He softened and began to relax at the walk.

This insistence is so simple to see and understand, yet so hard to accomplish for mere mortals with their horses. Think about it, can you consistently always be adamant a horse stays with you mentally and accept nothing less? It's not always easy to do when leading a quiet horse twenty feet, let alone when riding. And what about when the horse responds correctly to your cues mechanically speaking, keeping his thoughts with you, but without softness? Can you hold out further to get all the pieces of the puzzle you want in a horse at one time? If you're looking for a horse to be right on with your requests *and* reacting in a relaxed way, then you'll need to build that in there too. I saw all this being woven together as Harry rode that horse backwards, forwards, in circles, and sideways.

Harry backed that horse about fifty times right off the bat, hardly getting forward fifty feet. Would I have the kind of tenacity it takes to stick it out that long for the horse? Maybe not. Sometimes the idea that I want to *ride* (that is having a preconceived plan to saddle up and do something in particular) carries its own gravity and short circuits spending the kind of energy it takes to sort out these other incredibly important fundamentals. Plus, when I spend the time to work on the basics, like with Harry backing this horse, I sometimes start to second guess myself after the first thirty times. I wonder if I missed the slightest try fifteen times ago and am building in the opposite of what I want. Or, I begin to think I am presenting the wrong thing altogether.

I am improving at this sort of thing, though. I think I'm getting closer to the kind of knowledge that sometimes allows for the confidence that what I'm presenting is right and the horse will come through, eventually. That's why Harry enjoys the means to offer such a relentless insistence to the horse—he *knows* that horse is going to make it through to where he wants him to be...eventually.

The situation in the arena reminds me of how Harry often

just stands there in a round pen literally waiting on a horse to come through to a new understanding. This is so unlike many people who feel the need to be constantly pushing and driving on the horse, but rarely ever waiting. While riding the Morgan, Harry was quite busy, but at the same time he also was waiting on him in another sense. When he backed the horse, in essence he held out for the mind to come around and be present so a change would be possible. Then, once the horse made it, Harry would release and ask gently for whatever he was looking for, like a nice easy step forward—fully conscious, relaxed, with him, perfect. He kept insisting, and he finally got it. Then he made sure it stuck, and went on to something else.

Catherine works with Heyson on the ground before passing him off to Harry. (Tom Moates)

Harry knows when the horse is or is not with him. That's not always completely clear to me. Then again, the presentation of the backing (or whatever technique is chosen to snap back the horse's thought to the rider) must be of a particular timing and feel to avoid being punitive. Punish the horse, and resentment builds in.

Now for the really confusing part: all the time Harry is insisting on the horse's focus and getting a softening feel and relaxed step, he still presents the horse with choices. "Insisting" in the way I use the term here means Harry gets big enough to produce the need for the horse to make a choice (the horse is present mentally and realizes he must do something different). Then, Harry lets the horse make choices. When the "wrong" one is made, he doesn't prevent the horse from making it, but lets him experience that and puts enough pressure on the horse in some way to say, "See, that's not going to work out so well." All the while, Harry tries to set it up so the horse can easily find the "right" choice.

The beauty of the deal Harry offers, as I watched unfold with the Morgan, is that the right choice has an inherent aspect of naturally causing the horse to feel better anyway. Not just taking a step forward and walking straight, for example, but doing so relaxed. Of course that's going to feel better to the horse than taking a choppy forward step while feeling all pinched up inside. But how many horses are stuck with the latter? One must wonder, if one choice feels better than another, why doesn't the horse find it on his own more often?

I think humans mess it up for them. After watching Harry for many years now, I'm increasingly convinced it's up to us to realize we build the trouble into them. If we can see how we do that, then we can present things in such a way to the horse that we not only build in the control we need to ride a horse safely, but also insist on the silver lining—that the horse, when he chooses to go along with our way of thinking, always discovers, "Ah yes, that feels good!"

Harry rode that Morgan around the arena once they got to going, with the horse attentive and more relaxed than before. The horse worked up a sweat. Part of the difference in this kind of work is the amount of movement involved. Harry rode, occasionally backed and stopped, but a communication took place on many levels constantly as the ride progressed. The horse began to be able to bend through his whole body in a way not seen before as they turned in each direction at a committed walk. The Morgan was increasingly engaged to requests, yet softening to the rein. I observed the head position began to lower and stretch out. The head began to more readily tuck a little (give) to slight rein pressure—something along the lines of a "half-halt" or "picking up a soft feel." The horse became increasingly ready to hear anything Harry said with the reins and his body, and likewise positioned himself in a balanced way to receive a request when Harry gave a slight indication he might ask something.

Soon, Harry asked the horse to move up to the trot. It worried the Morgan. Harry backed him, and started over. Again, I witnessed the complete commitment Harry had to get all the aspects of the horse improving and feeling better as they entered new territory. Such consistency across the spectrum, it seemed to me then, is very practical for getting the horse into better shape. It's all related, feet, legs, back, head, mind, rider's position, rider's awareness, and on and on. That's what this example provided me that isn't as evident when something more focused in being worked on. I watched all these things coming together and improving at once.

Before long, the gelding was making the transition to the trot in a more relaxed way. Then they trotted all over, with Harry getting the horse increasingly soft at that faster speed. I even got to see a lovely impromptu "pot of dirt."

Another rider happened to be trotting along in the arena, and Harry came up trotting beside her, both horses in perfectly

Harry on Heyson making it look so simple. (Tom Moates)

synchronous steps, and said, "Look, we're doing a 'pot of dirt!'" (That's cowboy for "pas de deux," the ballet term for a duet, literally meaning a "step of two," which also is used in dressage for two horses performing together that mirror each others' moves to music.) I could almost hear Tchaikovsky's Swan Lake.

Harry had a similar experience going from the trot to the lope. He worked until the transitions and lope shaped up like the slower gaits.

Afterwards, the group discussed what unfolded there with Harry and the Morgan. Many of the changes described above were pointed out, and pretty clear. Then Harry made the point that while folks seemed to think a great deal of work went into the session, it only amounted to about forty-five minutes. That amount of time, in terms of a ride for most in the group, constituted a pretty short ride. How true. The time was relative to the task. The length of the ride wasn't impressive, rather it was the intensity of the work and pretty profound changes that occurred with the horse that made it seem like a long ride.

The owner went straight to the horse when Harry dismounted and climbed in the saddle. She knew from watching that she wanted to experience her horse right then, just after the Harry tune-up. She said so, and grinned wide as she felt her horse in that moment, soft and responsive like never before.

I like to see this kind of work and reflect on it often. I can't get it all effectively functioning for me, but I can try to get more of the pieces together as my horsemanship improves. Perhaps, even more important than getting all the steps together like Harry did that day with the Morgan, is the mindset this example represents. If we begin where we want to end up, not just in individual cues, but in the overarching approach to communicating with our horses, then we may better serve those horses by insisting they not only get what we're asking, but follow through in their work in a soft way that increases a comfortable mindset. The calm mind is more responsive and quick to hear what we have to say than the tight, worried mind.

Chapter 10

(Terry McCoy)

Wow!

Putting a couple bumps with my legs against a horse to help get him mentally and physically past the gate in a round pen (one of those thought magnets I mentioned earlier) wasn't an unusual practice for me by this time. New found confidence had grown in me. As a result, I enjoyed more matter-of-factness in the way I worked with horses than ever before.

Bump, bump. "Stay with me mentally, horse," I'd think. "Stay briskly walking and thinking forward on that line I'm projecting out there...." And off we'd go.

Except for this time. Instead of off we go, *off I went*!

It was during a horsemanship Bible camp with Harry and Ronnie Moyer, the first one Carol and I hosted in Floyd, Virginia. That year (2009), I was one of the week's six riders. I brought Jubal to ride for three of the five days. It was the first time he'd been out in the world since coming to our place from El Paso. I also planned to ride Carol's leopard Appaloosa gelding, Stoney, for the other couple of the days so she could see what Harry thought of him.

The crowd wrapped up and ducking behind the vehicles out of the wind at the round pen during a horsemanship/Bible clinic in Floyd, Virginia. (Terry McCoy)

Stoney, had proven to be the kind of horse that you chose out of your herd to put a kid on if anybody visited. The horse seemed unperturbed, never showing outward signs of acting up with Carol or others when ridden. Not to mention that, being covered from head to toe with copious black spots on a white coat base, he is a magnificent creature to behold. I'd been on him just a few times in the round pen in the couple years she'd owned him. It seemed to me he wasn't the most responsive horse on the farm, but came to Carol as a basic mainstream trail horse of a type that tended to stop in his tracks if things got a little confusing rather than go. Not a bad trait, really,

The first day of the clinic I worked Jubal loose in the round pen. The second day, Harry offered to work Stoney off of Jubal. I'd been very keen to have a chance to see Harry work one horse from another, and had been badgering him about it for awhile. Some years before I had seen Harry work horses from a saddle horse and I wanted to learn how to do it. When he suggested using Jubal to work Stoney to the group, I jumped at the chance, and was glad the others at the clinic agreed and were interested in it as well.

So, Harry rode Jubal and worked Stoney on lead. He demonstrated how to get the horses walking a circle head to tail and then bring Stoney through to walking parallel beside Jubal. Then I took his place on Jubal and gave it a try. I really stunk at it, but it was so much fun trying to get it right that I couldn't stop the jovial laughter that kept spilling out of me, and grinned ear to ear anyway.

By mid week, it started to look like I might just make it through a clinic as a rider without a big fat mishap. That would be a first. (The previous two, both with Niji, were a wreck where the

Keeper, a Paint Horse gelding, expresses his feelings with Harry and Jubal close by in the round pen in Tennessee. (Tom Moates)

saddle and I both were thrown, and the bolting incident, respectively.)

The next day I saddled up Stoney without any trouble in the round pen to get started riding him this time, and climbed aboard. Harry, Carol, and probably a dozen other clinickers were watching from a line of chairs set up beside a truck and trailer used as a windbreak just outside the round pen. I sat there on Stoney talking to Harry for a minute. Then I started from where the clump of humans were huddled together on one side of the pen and headed clockwise along the curved fence at a nice walk.

We made it half way around the pen, just opposite the spectators, when we encountered the gate. This gate might have been a thought magnet on its own, but since the round pen was situated within a large outdoor arena, Jubal happened to be loose just on the other side of the gate, amplifying the magnetism of that spot for Stoney.

I felt the drag in the gelding as his mind drew hard outside the pen. It was not surprising, and confidently, reflexively, I gave a quick, bump, bump.

Boom! That little spotty horse bucked like a mule. That particular acrobatic maneuver never had shown up in him before with a human aboard.

I distinctly remember bumping him with my legs, then the sharp buck, then the launch over the dashboard and through the windshield off to the left, then the flying through the air, and then the crash landing. There I was, in the dirt on my hands and knees, thrown clear of the saddle and the horse. I remember looking over at the sea of surprised and concerned faces through the fence panels. I managed to speak, but only a single word—a very slow and drawn out, "Wow!"

Relief clearly overcame the crowd when I said it, because laughter erupted (or maybe it was just really funny). I remained there in a dog-like position on all fours for another moment collecting my senses. Then I got up and brushed myself off, completely stunned that Stoney of all horses had just took to bucking like that. Next I figured there was no avoiding putting this incident in the next book as I slowly walked around to make sure all my parts still worked like they should.

Stoney's sudden strange bucking episode was so out of character that it presented lots of questions. I felt that the gelding was sort of shut down from the way his life had gone before coming our way. A horse in that mental state can be "bombproof" by mainstream standards, but if you begin to present him with choices in a Harry fashion and he starts to open up, sometimes the opinions you find are not quite what you hoped for! I think that may have factored into the situation. Of course, since it was such a bizarre and violent change for Stoney, we kicked around the possibilities that there could be a saddle issue, some soreness, that perhaps the change of coming to the clinic had triggered a new mental state we didn't get to at home, and so on.

Harry worked with Stoney to explore the gelding's (how shall we say it?) new found talent. Eventually he got on Jubal and ponied Stoney with Ronnie on the gelding's back to explore the situation for awhile. (I began to wonder if Ronnie gets the job of test pilot a lot at Bible clinics?) The gelding seemed like he had some buck in him still from where I sat watching, but Harry stayed ahead of it and Ronnie kept petting the horse's neck and reassuring him as they rode around. The gelding really came around quickly with those two working with him. Even I was riding him again before the end of the clinic, and doing pretty well. Carol, however, very naturally was now dubious of Stoney, where before she had been completely confident.

Over the winter Stoney was kept close to home in one of our valley pastures with a couple other horses. That winter was one of the worst in memory here in the Blue Ridge Mountains. Very little happened on the farm beyond just trying to keep the basics going, like plowing the snow and ice off the road, feeding, watering, and getting in firewood. Stoney didn't get worked with at all.

When spring finally came around, Carol and I both had

Stoney pop to the forefront of our minds. His situation with the bucking incident remained unresolved, and we both had ruminated on the fall clinic for many months. Increasingly I was convinced that bucking me off was related both to the gelding's awakening from a life shut down at the hands of those who had ridden him before, and perhaps my abrupt request to get him forward (mentally and physically). Carol wanted to see him ridden to decide just what kind of horse she really had on her hands. I offered to bring him into the round pen and just start off slowly on the ground and see what we found. So we did.

A rope halter and long lead rope were on Stoney when we started off. Just to check in with him, I stood behind his shoulder on his left side and gently asked with my left hand on the lead rope for him to bend his head and bring his thought around my way. The horse would not do it. He remained board straight and rigid. Then he tried to step towards me (on me, actually) to relieve the pressure of me asking him to bend.

Aha! That was pretty dog gone clear, I thought. Then I wondered if I had missed this the year before? I must have. There was no way he developed this rigidity in one winter, turned out with a few other horses. We played with that a little on both sides and it was *terrible*! The worst I had ever seen, and I marveled that I must have missed it in him before. I have to wonder about myself sometimes, but it's like Harry says, "Until you see it, you can't see it, and then when you do, you wonder how you never saw it before." Chalk up another one for Harry.

I spent over an hour the first day just getting Stoney to begin giving to a little feel on the lead rope. I'd try to break his thought loose by asking for a bend and then holding out, and settled for even a hint of a bend at first. Fifteen minutes passed and I wasn't getting it much better. By the end of that first go around it did improve, but not by great leaps. The left side freed up more easily than the right. The gelding would look around that way when I asked and bend a couple of inches at least. Also, he stopped trying to step over to the

Tom, on Jubal, works with Stoney during a clinic in Floyd, Virginia. (Terry McCoy)

left as the willingness to bend increased. On the right, just getting him to bring a thought around and look my way was challenging, and he kept up the desire to stay completely rigid and step on me.

Later, I heard Harry discussing this very same sided-ness issue at another clinic. He explained that in horses with this situation, while they bend better to the left, they actually turn better to the right. I found this to be exactly the case with Stoney, and remember thinking how counterintuitive it was. (I actually was pretty stoked I'd had the wherewithal to discover it on my own and then hear Harry describe it later.) Harry said that a horse readily moves his feet on the side where he'd *really* rather not offer any bend as a way to avoid bending, just like Stoney, which translates into a pretty quick turn to that direction. On the other side, they bend better and are typically more reluctant to move their feet.

The second day that I worked with Stoney is when this became more clear. I put Carol's roping saddle on him, along with a bridle with a snaffle bit this time rather than the halter, and then went through asking him to bend in each direction from the ground like the day before. It went about the same as what we'd ended up with the previous day. Remembering very well our past bucking experience, I took plenty of time fooling around with the saddle, stirrups, and stepping up with one foot in them on each side before I threw a leg over the horse and sat there.

Then I made a pledge to myself and Stoney that at first I would not worry about whether or not he moved. I would concentrate only on getting a bend in his neck and his thought to come around, and release for that. If he wanted to walk or trot or stand still or back up, I would not address any of that yet. I'd just sit up there and hold onto my request regarding the bend and not fuss about the feet, which at this stage were far less important to me than just getting some softness and responsiveness in this horse.

This was new territory for me, and might be called "terror-tory" to tell the truth, since it meant surrendering control I'd typically much rather have. We were in a round pen, so it wasn't like he could go far. Of course, I've told myself this before and have been plenty uncomfortable with a horse out of control in a round pen, but this time I was resigned not to worry about that. Instead, I'd sit in the saddle only concerned with asking for his head and neck to bend. Then I'd release when it happened, and the horse's thought also came through. I'd like to see the bend come through the body, but for now this first baby step was my goal.

The plan was surprisingly successful. At first he stood perfectly still and very braced up, but I was able to get the left side giving a little bit. Things progressed, with a lot if bit chomping, and sure enough before long he added forward motion to his attempts to get away from my requests on the reins to bend. I stuck to my guns and just focused on the bend and the thought coming around to the request, and went along with all the rest of whatever he did. After walking around all over the place, especially near the gate, he came through with a try (a slight giving to the rein pressure on a side) and I released. Soon, I tried to spend all the awareness I could muster on watching for both the physical motion *and* the commitment to thinking around to that side before releasing. I didn't want to just teach Stoney a rubber-necking maneuver to avoid my request on the rein while continuing to have his mind truly committed to some other agenda of his own.

That's how things went for several days with slow but observable improvement in his willingness to think around to the side and bend when asked. The bit chomping lessened. The next day during our work, though, he added trotting to his unhindered movements for the first time. I still just let him move about however he needed to and worked on that bending request until I got a change.

Not insisting on a stop and allowing the horse to go wherever he chose while I was in the saddle proved very uncomfortable for me mentally. Especially at first when he was quite amped up and really asserting his mind about the situation. It seemed initially he even packed an expectation of an eminent rider intervention as part of his anxiety. When it didn't come, his overall electric buzz of weirdness dialed back quite a bit, and he became able to better sort out this one thing I was doing—simply putting a little feel on a single rein.

Working on controlling his general movements at that time, I figured, would hinder any progress on the task at hand. Splitting what focus he had into too many scattered requests might dilute the work on bending and add to Stoney's confusion as he tried to sort out these new and troubling interactions I presented. Consistency was essential for true progress, and it was way easier for me to be consistent doing one thing so my own focus didn't wander as well.

Likewise, boxing Stoney in by blocking his feet with the bit seemed a recipe for increasing his ill feelings. Besides, I needed to get a bend working to have the horse disengage all the way through his body to the hind quarters, mentally and physically, to get a real stop anyway. This all seemed connected, and it felt like we were on the right track.

Working with Stoney from the saddle this way reminded me of one reason using a round pen can be effective. The round corral allows a person to remain in close proximity to work with a loose horse even with the horse moving around. Being in the saddle worked really well in this same kind of way since it allowed me to just be right there on the horse and make very consistent requests and releases with the reins. The riding position provided me the opportunity to be always in the same place in reference to the bit and Stoney's head and neck, regardless of where and how he moved around.

It is amazing to me that a horse like Stoney is so convinced that bending is threatening. This horse was incredibly attached to keeping his body rock rigid and arrow straight. The significance of being in that state (probably his way of being like a cocked gun ready to shoot out of there at any second to flee for his life) I think can be hard for the human to fully comprehend. It seemed to me all I was doing was asking him to bend his neck and bring his head around just a little at first. The way he interpreted that situation must have been extremely disturbing for him to be so unwilling to do so for so long.

The second day of working from the saddle went much better than the first. Especially to the left, Stoney began to bring his thought and head around more willingly. His neck softened, as did the muscles in his top line as the motion in his body freed up some. By the third day, I was firming up and bringing each rein further around and getting the hind quarters stepping over.

In all the time I'd been working with Stoney, I sensed that if I had asked him to go forward with a little leg pressure, he would have bucked like at the clinic. I don't know for sure, but it felt that way to me then and I was careful not to do it.

In the midst of working Stoney those few days in the saddle, he did a lot of walking at different speeds around the round pen. The bending improved to the point that I began to take the opportunity to arc him into a small circle when he walked, as Harry had me do with Niji in the past. Before long, I worked on spiraling him down until he stopped, and then released.

On the third day as we worked, the gelding even went trotting around the pen of his own accord. By this time my own confidence in letting the horse just go forward if he needed to had improved to the point that it neither startled nor bothered me. We went to trotting, I rode it just fine, and then asked for an arc. We wound down to a walk, then a tighter circle, and eventually disengaged the

Ronnie on Stoney, and Harry on Jubal, enjoying themselves in Floyd, Virginia. (Terry McCoy)

hind quarters, stopped, and I released the rein.

This kind of progress with Stoney felt fantastic. Here was a project with a horse I'd begun which possessed uncertain results for sure. Yet, I'd found a spot right away where there was some trouble, and began getting small improvements. Then, over time, I had helped bring about some clear progress with extremely good results. Perhaps just as important as Stoney's observable improvement was my own new found ability to go with the horse and help support him on the move from the saddle.

The ultimate reward from working with this horse for me came next, and was two fold. First, I finally got around to asking Stoney to go forward. This I did extremely gently, with little more than me thinking about putting a little leg pressure on him along with me upping the forward energy in my body. The time must have been right, because he was happy to do it. It was smooth and unbothered. From then on, asking for a walk went well, and before long I carefully asked for a trot and got a gentle transition into one there as well.

Second, Carol observed much of the work we did, and felt confidence again in Stoney. When a horse suddenly gives a dangerous or disturbing behavior, it can really take the wind out of the owner's sails. I know I felt knotted up about the bucking at the clinic, and felt uncertain about what would or should happen next with the gelding. Being able to have the ability to at least search and improve the horse's condition to some extent, and get back to riding with a feeling of safety and confidence, at least in the round pen for starters, is hard to beat.

Chapter 11

(Tom Moates)

The Razor's Edge Revisited

"The Razor's Edge" is a term I use for that very delicate mental threshold where a horse teeters on the verge of losing it when presented with something he finds distressing. It's also the name of a chapter in my previous book, *A Horse's Thought.* It discusses how sometimes the human must confront a horse with the very things that disturb him and allow the angst to rise to a high level before it becomes possible to convince the horse to view those situations differently. Pushing a horse to the brink of trouble may be the only way to enable the horse to make new choices about the circumstances and provide the opportunity for a new and positive outcome. Horses live in the moment, so the problem must be brought into the moment to be addressed. Harry is a master at this.

Loreli, a mare owned by Rita and Andy Riddile (they own Little Cove Farm in Saint Leonard, Maryland: www.littlecovefarm.com), provided the perfect example of what I hoped to convey in that previous chapter. The chestnut Hanoverian, with a blaze, and socks on her hind feet, is a tall athlete and a real handful for anyone on the other end of the lead rope if she gets the notion to leave town. She used to get that notion quite a lot when triggered by certain situations—like when around a flag, or especially anything going on above her head. Otherwise, the mare seemed to be quite sweet and reasonable.

Nearly two years after the clinic discussed in that chapter in the previous book, I was lucky enough to witness Loreli make further breakthroughs with Harry's help during a two week stay at another clinic at Mendin' Fences Farm in Tennessee in 2010. Again, it perfectly illustrated how the razor's edge must be approached sometimes to help a troubled horse. Following her progress provides an outstanding opportunity to see specific work and resulting changes in a horse with Harry's help over quite a long period of time.

There is no question that Harry got profound changes in Loreli, well beyond what I had seen before in the mare, in a short time at this recent clinic. I'm likewise convinced that long term and consistent work done by Rita with the mare between clinics laid the ground work for the changes I witnessed there when Harry got working with her. Ultimately, it is a pleasure to revisit Loreli's story and share a little more on the idea of the razor's edge. This is especially true since I spoke with Rita after her return home and took down some of her direct thoughts about both the clinic and how Loreli is doing now that she's been reintroduced back home for several weeks.

Rita Riddile with Loreli in Tennessee. (Tom Moates)

A major part of the example Loreli provides is showing that the timing to know when to dial up and down the pressure—to bring up the level of trouble in the horse and then present things in such a way that a change for the better results—is very tricky. I call the balancing point of what the horse can and can't take "the razor's edge" because it is such a fine line between a horse being troubled but coping with something, or tipping over the edge into a complete melt down where panic, fight, or flight can make a bad situation much worse.

Harry on Jubal introducing his hat to Loreli. (Tom Moates)

To complicate matters, it's a moving target. For example, Loreli was very sensitive to the flag around her head the first week of the recent Tennessee clinics and it would take very little pressure from it to send her bolting away. By the middle of the second week, the point of overload and panic when presented with a flag in the same way was in a very different place—it's not that she could "take" more, but rather that she genuinely felt more at ease around more pressure from the flag and *experienced* it in an altogether different, more positive way. Even during the course of working with a horse on this kind of thing the razor's edge moves around, sometimes from minute to minute.

I know from watching Harry for years now that he does not just present tough scenarios to horses and remove them randomly hoping for a change. He also does not "pressure and release" the presentation of such things for simple surface changes in a horse, which may be considered well timed by others' standards, and even seemingly produce better behavior in the horse. Harry knows what deeper change he seeks in the horse and (by golly) he sticks it out until that better feeling starts to come in there, regardless of what else is going on, before letting up. I can watch him do that with a horse, recognize what I see with clarity, and still not be very handy with it myself when I'm working with a troubled horse.

Generally speaking, I have seen "sacking-out," or "desensitizing," demonstrations done by many different people where desensitizing is not synonymous with a real positive transformation in the horse's thinking and feeling. Rather, all too often the horse gets boxed in by the process. He is made to understand he must tolerate the spooky thing or he'll be in even worse trouble from the human than he experienced from the thing in the first place.

"Making the right thing easy, and the wrong thing difficult," can have this effect when neither of those things makes the horse feel better inside about the situation. The person must create an opportunity that allows the horse to come to a better feeling and understanding about what has been troubling him for it *to be an option.* That's sounds pretty basic, but so many times a horse isn't provided the choice to feel better on the menu, so he just picks the best he can.

Enduring trouble is not feeling better or being convinced that things are really alright, but is simply stuffing the bad feelings. The technique of presenting and removing troubling things to the horse can produce varying results depending on the timing and handling of the process. The different ways of handling this may appear all the same to the onlooker if the nuances of bringing a horse through to a better place aren't truly understood.

Harry presents trouble, and does so at a level the horses can handle even if it is right up against the razor's edge. Sometimes it seems a horse needs to be brought to that level of intensity to produce the willingness to search for another answer and break the old habit. Then Harry waits for a positive change to come into the horse's mind before providing relief and starting again. In the past, experience proved decidedly to the horse that this negative reaction he uses works to rid himself of the dreadful thing, whatever it is. He is absolutely sure of it. He may go to great lengths to hold on to that thought. Loreli showed this over and over by suddenly and rather fiercely bolting away from flags, hats, and such things. If she became nervous about the flag, she departed the scene so strongly it was nearly impossible at times to hold the lead rope and bring her back around to reassess the situation.

The positive change is a result of the horse wanting to be rid of the trouble in the first place (a natural tendency), discovering that the old method to do so for some reason isn't working now (the person keeps presenting the trouble even as the horse attempts to get rid of it in the old way—not always fun), and thus is being made to search for some new way to find relief from it (since the old method doesn't work anymore, what can be done about it now?).

That new search is brought on by the trouble being present in a sufficient degree and duration to break the old thought. Then, the human must recognize when the thought changes from the habit of the negative to the direction of the positive as the horse seeks to cope. The release from it must be timed to this new direction of thinking to get the horse to recognize and build on the new thoughts: relaxing, looking to the human for comfort, and accepting the situation as generally okay.

I first saw Loreli with Rita at Mendin' Fences Farm in Tennessee in 2008. The mare absolutely panicked at the flag and other fluttery things. In particular, anything above her head, such as a person sitting on top of a fence panel, set her off. In that clinic her anxiety about these things overwhelmed her to the point of tearing the lead rope away from Rita and running off in the arena on a few occasions. I remember in particular an afternoon where I held her lead rope through a fence panel in the outdoor arena keeping her facing me. Harry, some fifteen feet away at least, held a flag gently and walked slowly behind her one way and then the other. This switched the clinician from one of Loreli's eyes to the other. Even that exercise, with Harry quite a distance away, nearly pushed the mare beyond the razor's edge at that time.

When I next saw Loreli and Rita it was in Hanover, Virginia at a week long clinic later that year. The experience spelled out in the previous book first involved having folks simply sitting on the round pen panels and slowly getting Loreli to feel better about being in the pen with that. Then she eventually was lead closer to people, and finally felt the confidence to put her nose out and smell them. Eventually she was exposed to some people very carefully holding flags up there. By the end of the week she could be led through a tight gauntlet of us on the ground touching her with flags and still remain relaxed. That's a really boiled down version, but allows for a pretty easily understood physical representation of how the mare felt at first, and how much better things were for her to be able to take standing in a cluster of flags relaxed by the end. It was a huge change for her, but the same troubles remained embedded in her and bubbled to the surface at times.

I next saw Loreli and Rita at Mendin' Fences in 2010. The mare was not nearly as skittish as before, but that same kind of worry remained in her, and she wasn't beyond some very strong reactions at times still. Clearly the trouble with noise and movement up over her, especially around her head, seemed to get her right up against the razor's edge in a hurry.

Harry borrowed Jubal to ride as a saddle horse that year in Tennessee, and he used Jubal with Loreli on several occasions. I watched intently one day as he flagged Loreli from Jubal. Later, he worked the mare from Jubal on a lead rope, which seemed to go really well overall, but if Harry reached up and touched his cowboy hat—especially if his hand made a sound on the hat—the mare became extremely troubled and fled abruptly. Once Harry realized this, the hat became a major prop in the drama that unfolded over the rest of the clinic with her.

When Harry finds a thing that presses a horse up to that flash point, he seems to view it as a very valuable tool to get the horse working through those tough spots. Over and over across many days he removed his hat and presented it to Loreli to get her increasingly convinced her ill feelings about it don't need to be. I think many of the other less troubling problems of this type may even evaporate to some extent in the process of working on the big things. Of course, Rita knows this mare better than anybody, and I asked her about what unfolded in those weeks with Harry.

"I think that this was the third or forth time that Harry's actually worked with her in this way, where he brought up a very high level of worry and got her to understand that it was okay," Rita told me. "That all of that worry could come up and that she was not going to die. He's done that with her from the ground before, and that was very scary for her, but her largest area of fear is from up above. Like the hat kind of thing, or being up on the panels. He did work with her some on that before, but this time it was almost exclusively working from above her—flagging her from on top of the panels coming down towards her back, down towards her head. I don't know if you even could have done that with her a year and a half ago. She was more ready inside to be able to handle and reach the place that she did this year. And then, on top of all of that, is his [Harry's] ability to understand and to go there, to bring up that worry, and at the same time not confirm that the horse has anything to be afraid of. It's his gift. It's certainly something I've never seen anyone else do. His ability to bring up those issues in a horse and let the horse know it's okay at the same time."

Loreli is clearly a complex horse. She's smart and quick and big, but she also shows the capacity and desire to try and sort things out. I felt pretty certain as I watched her over a couple weeks there that she strained mentally to meet Harry half way with the work he did. Horses don't deliberately act up. She couldn't help it when the pressure became too much for her and her past experiences dictated her reactions. But, as scared as she was, she still wanted to see if she could trust Harry and find a better deal even with some very spooky stuff going on between them. I expect that big heartedness in this mare may have a lot to do with why Rita has been so attached to her, and worked so hard over time to help her get to a truly better spot.

At one point, with Harry standing on a box outside the round pen working the mare on a lead rope with his hat, she tipped over the mental edge and bolted, snatched the rope from his hand, and got loose in the round pen. Even with that over-exposure to the wrong side of the razor's edge, Loreli quickly recovered with Harry and was back working on the hat deal again. She rebounded way better than what I had witnessed with her in the past. Before long she was relaxing much more as Harry rubbed the hat on her face, ears, and neck. He even set it up there making her look quite silly as if she was wearing it.

I have to admit, seeing that situation and knowing Harry sometimes goes past the razor's edge and loses grip on a horse left me feeling a little comforted—that if it does happen sometimes even to Harry, maybe it's not the end of the world. That there is still the chance to pick up and go on with the work of getting things better with the horse. Sometimes I suffer from spilt milk syndrome: worrying about what has already occurred that I can't do anything about now. An example like this makes me feel more ready to pick up the lead rope and start again rather than become paralyzed and agonize over what just happened that I can't change now anyway.

"I don't have the ability, the judgment, and the timing to bring up the level of worry that Harry does and then let the horse come back down," Rita said, when we discussed the clinic after it was over. "I don't get her as worried as he does. By worried I mean presenting her with a situation that she's very uncomfortable with. I do that at home. I get up on the panels. I do flag her. I do thump around with the saddle. I ask her to do things that she is worried about doing. I do all of that, but I am not capable of doing it at the same level that he is. That year and a half that I've owned her we've been working on those things—there hasn't been any big wrecks and no physical true threat to her—but I could not do what he did, which was really go in there to the heart of what she was feeling.

"He brings that in there, but he doesn't leave it there. And my confidence in my own ability is not that great, that if I brought up that level of worry, that when it was over I wouldn't leave some of it in there. I don't do it at the level that he does it, but I certainly do it at the level that I'm confident with. And we do all those things, it's just, as you well know, you think you're doing it and then you hand the lead rope over to Harry and it does not look the same!"

To my delight, I caught many days where Harry rode Jubal and worked other horses in the Tennessee clinics that year. One of my favorites was when he and Jubal were in the round pen with Rita on her big Hanoverian mare, Brighid, and together they sandwiched Loreli.

All three horses were in the round pen that Thursday morning of Loreli's second week of clinic. Harry was on Jubal, wearing chaps and a cowboy hat, and using his western slick fork saddle. Loreli and Brighid had English saddles on. Loreli was in a rope halter and lead rope. First, Rita flagged Loreli from the ground as Harry watched from atop Jubal and Brighid just hung out. It went very well. Then Harry worked Loreli from Jubal for awhile. Harry began by circling the two horses head to tail. This is a move where he gets a bend in Jubal and rides him in the circle he wants while he leads Loreli's head towards Jubal's tail so they get in synch as two halves of a circle. Then Harry changes the feel on the lead rope and brings his arm forward so that as they are walking the circle, Jubal continues and Loreli brings her body around and her front end comes through. She ends up walking head to head with Jubal in parallel. She was a little sticky at times, but not terrible, and improved with Harry's coaching and encouraging words.

"Come on little mare," he'd say. (She was taller than Jubal.) "Come on little mare."

As things got better with the circling deal, I notice Harry increasingly reaching over to pet Loreli on the neck, and eventually taking more opportunities to rub around her head where so much of her angst originates.

Then Rita threw a leg over Brighid. Harry and Jubal rode on the inside of the round pen ponying Loreli, and Rita and Brighid rode along the outside making a Loreli sandwich. They double teamed the mare, petting her, rubbing on her, and they had a pair of stuffed riding pants which they used as a mock lower half of a human to throw over the saddle and around her neck for another way to present something akin to the feeling of a rider to add into the mix. Then they changed direction which put Harry and Jubal on the outside track and Rita and Brighid on the inside. Harry got a big smile on his face as the session went extremely well. The scenario worked to support Loreli with both horses, which provided both comfort and a platform for two people to present a lot of overhead activity.

Rita stopped and dismounted. Harry went back to presenting his hat from above to Loreli while sitting on Jubal. Words can't present the kind of change I sensed in this horse at that time. Simply saying something like, "Loreli relaxed and improved, blah...blah," doesn't even hint at the deep change that unfolded inside this mare at the end of the second week of clinics that time. It was as if Harry and Rita finally figured out the cure for a parasite that had ailed the horse, and they killed off those buggers leaving the mare happy

Rita on Brighid, and Harry on Jubal, sandwich Loreli between them. (Tom Moates)

and healthy. When Loreli left she'd have been contented to wear a cowboy hat.

"The plan is to continue doing all of these things," Rita reports from back home in Maryland. "Now I can flag her much more aggressively from over the panels, from up on top of her, banging on the saddle—do all of that stuff way more aggressively because she's not as worried. So I don't have to worry about scrambling around and her getting loose. But...I don't want her to forget or think that it was an anomaly that it happened. Or that it only happens in Tennessee. I don't want there to be an association with a specific location or person [Harry] because this horse compartmentalizes so many things. So I want to try to convey to her that this is a broader experience than just that one time in that one place with that one person.

"I'm being particularly guarded. And I don't mean that I'm tip-toeing, but I am making sure that since right now the horse is so vulnerable in a way that she wasn't before, because she just trusts that everything is going to be okay, I don't put her in a position that something's going to happen to her. As many days a week as I can I'm doing these things with her to try and make this a permanent change. That she understands that this is it. This is the way it could be. This is the way it will be."

The horsemanship journey for one seeking to improve is never over. No matter how much we learn, or how much we accomplish with horses, there is always more to be discovered. Coming back to revisit Loreli and Rita further along their journey together provides an example of this on many levels. It shows how tough it can be to work through an issue with a horse; that it can take years of persistent searching, learning, and positive interaction with some horses to get to a significant breakthrough. It shows that such breakthroughs are indeed possible. Seeing Loreli's progress at that recent clinic illustrated to me all over again how the person must sometimes go right up to the razor's edge to get the horse beyond his trouble. It also reminds me that presenting the right thing, at the right time, and in the right degree of intensity is very tricky at times, and if not understood properly can go badly and produce the opposite effect of what is desired.

I appreciate Rita for following through with Loreli, especially since there was never any guarantee that she would get a significant change for the better with this horse. Also, their story allows me to show how I've witnessed that getting to Harry's clinics, whether as a rider or an auditor, can produce real constructive transformation for horses and humans. Rita and Loreli improved at all three clinics where I saw them. I've come to a better understanding about how to get a horse to overcome trouble by being there some of the time to observe what took place, and I feel certain other onlookers have as well.

These clinics are condensed moments in time where Harry can guide such changes at a pretty rapid pace. By being so immersed in the clinic setting, a momentum develops that has a real capacity to alter our view of how to get horses feeling better about things, and help us to apply this new knowledge. Loreli stands out in my mind as living proof of this, especially after speaking with Rita about how the mare is doing since returning home.

"The difference is," Rita sums it up, "she's still quiet, but even when things start—people come in [the barn], and start feeding—

she's still very calm inside. [Before] you could see her, even when she was in her stall, or standing in the aisle, when that worry came up inside of her, she would bow up physically. So her feet would get closer together underneath her, she was ready to go somewhere, her back would tighten up, her neck would shorten and come back, her head would get high, and she's not doing *any* of that. It's amazing!

"Every time I'm with her it is almost a tightness in my chest where I go, 'This is a miracle!' It is so different from the way it was."

Chapter 12

(Tom Moates)

Faith

A discussion ensued recently between me and someone who had read my previous book, *A Horse's Thought.* She articulated great angst that, in retrospect, maybe she had done more damage than good to her horses over the years. The unfolding of some troubles of mine in the book, along with Harry's advice, left her feeling she might be better off leaving horses alone altogether.

Usually for me, it's when things go terribly wrong with a horse right in front of me that gives me a dreadful, "Oh no!" moment. Sometimes it results from my mistake that took a horse beyond the razor's edge and tipped him off the deep end. Other times, it is just a bad situation that develops from circumstances beyond my control, but there I am in the middle of it. Or, I've been known to miss some trouble in a horse and thereby gotten into a wreck which in turn I had to go back and sort out.

This horsewoman, however, had that wretched experience when she read about "riding the line." The idea is that we need to consistently support our horses and keep them mentally with us every step. She worried that she had missed a bunch of what was going on with her horses in the past, while enjoying trail rides in particular, and thus felt terribly irresponsible. I appreciated the chance to consider the dilemma she felt and comment on it. It's a concern that deserves some serious attention. And, I know she is not alone since others have spoken to me about having similar feelings at times.

Even though there may be some real grounds for this reaction in people, it is often pointless for folks to feel this way for several reasons. The first is that the kind of people who feel this way are the ones who deeply care about getting better with their horses. That crushing feeling in their chest is there because it is so important to them to improve the relationship between them and their horses. They are exactly the ones who *should* continue to work with horses, not quit!

Next, it is no accident that this dilemma is noticed by the people who are improving their horsemanship skills. It is in our improvement that we are able to realize things we've missed in the past. So, if it weren't for our progress in horsemanship, we'd never see what we might have done better at an earlier time, or feel guilty about it. This shouldn't be viewed in utter sadness, but rather seen as a natural by-product of our growth. It's a mile marker on the trail to better horsemanship.

Kathy Baker about to mount Ari in Tennessee. (Tom Moates)

Then there is the question of a horse's overall condition in life. Even someone who may not be the most handy horse person, but who is working to improve, is probably making progress and working through some of a horse's issues with humans. Certainly these kinds of owners care deeply about their horses. I see they tend to work hard to provide excellent attention to details like vet care, hoof care, and proper feed. They also tend to work towards a willing partner with a horse and want to steer away from depending on mechanical devices for control.

I've always done the best I could every step along the way with the equines in my life. Sure, Harry could have done it better, but he can't care for every horse. And, I see so many people trying hard to make the situation better for the horses in their care that I am very encouraged.

In these books I'm both sharing my own pitfalls with horses that triggered some growth, and trying to set a high water mark by sharing Harry's sage words and lessons. The chapters unfold to show some horsemanship progress either with me or in someone I observed. Clearly, these are not how-tos or some step by step program. Through these writings I hope to provide a window into some new ways of thinking that Harry helped me, or others, attain to bring about positive long term results when working with horses.

When we who seek to improve with horses are at a clinic, or read a book, or work with a horse at home and have a bit of growth in this area, it represents a change in us. Understanding commingles with responsibility, and, as stated above, we then realize what we *didn't* accomplish before we acquired this understanding. That can produce pangs of guilt, but it goes back to that saying I've quoted from Harry a ton of times, "Until we see it, we can't see it; then when we see it, we wondered how we never saw it before." But if we couldn't see it, then there is nothing we could have done about that then. It is fruitless to worry about it now, just keep the lesson in mind as you

Harry hanging out on Jubal in Tennessee. (Tom Moates)

go work with the horses you have today. They can benefit from your new understanding.

Trail riding is an example that came up in the recent conversation I mentioned, and it is a topic that comes up frequently when this subject is discussed. In riding a line, for example, you seek to have your horse with you continually. So, what if you're out riding along enjoying the day, talking to friends, and admiring the wonderful clouds against the blue sky? Is that wrong? Are you doing your horse a disservice?

I've talked to Harry about this very thing. His answer is that if you are on the trail riding along, and you check in with your horse and he's gone off mentally, then yes—stop looking at the sky and do what you must to get the horse back with you, and then proceed. If, however, you're riding along and you check in with your horse and he's right there for you, then sure, go ahead and check out the sky; just don't leave the horse in a void the whole time you're out riding. He also said that if the horse isn't fidgety, why mess with him? In other words, you can tell in many ways whether a horse is with you or not, and if he is going along nicely and feeling of you and you are feeling of him while the ride is going on, that's great.

I'm still learning and sorting this kind of thing out through my own experiences. Just this week I had a yearling filly I've been teaching to lead get pushed past the razor's edge one evening. It startled me since I didn't catch the reason she suddenly decided to spook and attempt to run away. The reaction was completely out of character for her. Luckily, the feel of the halter and lead rope along with her positive feelings for the human (I suppose) allowed me to run a little line out and then bend her around, disengage the hind quarters, and get her back with me pretty quickly. I felt then that my experience, and what I'd been capable of establishing with her in terms of our understanding to that point, helped us avert a crisis.

In the past, when I was less experienced, that horse might have gotten away from me, or I might have handled the rope all wrong and she could have become troubled enough to go over backwards—who knows. But, things went pretty well considering. A sense of fulfillment welled up in me about getting through that tough moment with her. A potentially bad situation came out okay, at least in part due to my experiences in learning to get better in horsemanship. There's only a few things that compare to that wonderful feeling, but it has taken plenty of the opposite feeling at times over the years to get here.

I think all serious students of Harry's recognize horses in our pasts that we could better help now. In a way I hope so, otherwise there's been no real progress in a person's horsemanship. Likewise, if you are experiencing the pangs of worry about messing up a horse in the past, you have developed your skills and understanding to gain that realization. If you continue to improve, then what you're up to now isn't as good as it'll be later, so the same will continue to hold true in the future.

One final note on this subject is that even with the bad situations I've gotten into, where I thought I had messed a horse up pretty bad, it hasn't held true. I'm reminded of Loreli ripping the rope from Harry's hands while he worked with her in the previous chapter, and how that wasn't the end of that story; he matter-of-factly went over and picked the lead rope up and proceeded to get a better change with the mare. He didn't cave in to worry—he just regrouped, like he always does, and kept at it. And it came out fine.

So far even I have been able to go back after many a misadventure and get things with those horses better again. Horses are incredibly flexible and forgiving creatures. It is amazing to see how much improvement can be made with them even in a short time when we avoid discouragement and continue to work to sort it out.

Harry rides Nan Barta's Quarter Horse, Worthy, at a clinic in Eagle Lake, Minnesota. (Tom Moates)

Developing faith that it can be done, that we can do this, and that the horse will get better, is such an important part of improving horsemanship. Oddly, faith in a positive outcome seems little discussed in the realm of horse work. That's probably because it can't be purchased like a piece of tack, or explained in a certain number of steps on a DVD, or shown in a series of photos. Still, it is a critical cornerstone to getting better with horses, and it is freely available to all who wish to develop it.

It is this faith that Harry just plain embodies. In him, it is like a beacon for the horse. I think the horse senses what Harry presents, in some horse way, saying, "Hey horse, try this. You will feel much better when you catch on to this choice I'm suggesting to you here."

I have witnessed so many horses helped that have come from extremely bad backgrounds, that I know how much they can come through to new understandings and get to feeling much better about life with humans. It is one of those great deals where there are no losers—the horses and the humans both benefit. It's worth all the work, even enduring the growing pains of missed opportunities and misunderstandings.

So, I'd like to wrap things up by just encouraging folks to weather the tough times. If I got through the wrecks and wrangles with horses I've gotten into and come out the other side with a better understanding, anybody can do it. Fulfillment comes from work, and if you focus on improving your horsemanship skills, have faith in a positive outcome, and don't forget to have fun along the way, the joy of success will be yours. And your horse's too, for that matter.

(Nan Barta)

About the Author

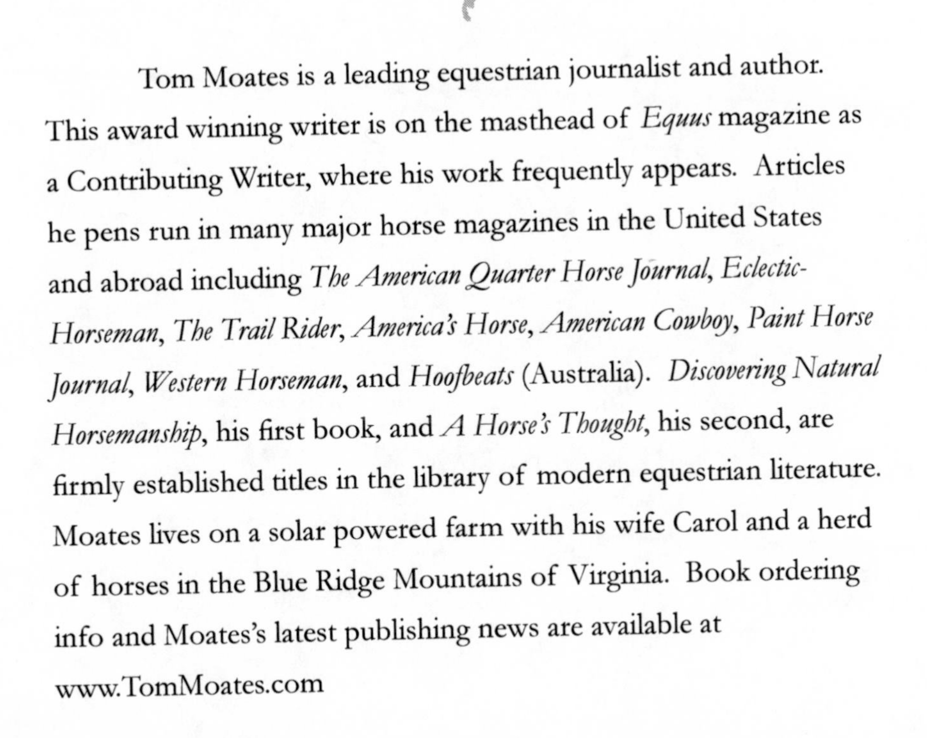

Tom Moates is a leading equestrian journalist and author. This award winning writer is on the masthead of *Equus* magazine as a Contributing Writer, where his work frequently appears. Articles he pens run in many major horse magazines in the United States and abroad including *The American Quarter Horse Journal*, *Eclectic-Horseman*, *The Trail Rider*, *America's Horse*, *American Cowboy*, *Paint Horse Journal*, *Western Horseman*, and *Hoofbeats* (Australia). *Discovering Natural Horsemanship*, his first book, and *A Horse's Thought*, his second, are firmly established titles in the library of modern equestrian literature. Moates lives on a solar powered farm with his wife Carol and a herd of horses in the Blue Ridge Mountains of Virginia. Book ordering info and Moates's latest publishing news are available at www.TomMoates.com

CPSIA information can be obtained at www.ICGtesting.com
Printed in the USA
LVOW040655081211

258251LV00002B/182/P